SOCIALISM
FOR THE DUMMIES

SOCIALISM
FOR THE DUMMIES

MICHAEL ENGMANN

Library of Congress Control Number: 2020913078
ISBN: Hardcover   978-1-6641-1989-5
                Softcover   978-1-6641-1990-1
                eBook   978-1-6641-1963-5

Print information available on the last page.

Rev. date: 07/30/2020

To order additional copies of this book, contact:
Xlibris
1-888-795-4274
www.Xlibris.com
Orders@Xlibris.com
816508

CONTENTS

INTRODUCTION

What is Democratic Socialism in America?

There are many interpretations of socialism. The consensus point is that the government will play the major role in running the economy and planning for its future. Therefore, the government will run and/ or own the major industries of the economy. The major premise underlying the socialistic philosophy is that the capitalistic system (individual ownership of society's businesses for profit) allows the private owners to exploit their workers by keeping working wages low and therefore enabling businesses to make excess profits for the owners. The owners become rich at the expense of the worker. And, the rich, not only have access to greater current resources, but their richness enables their offspring to have an unfair advantage over the rest of society in perpetuity. So, therefore the government has to control any excess profits by either owning the abusing companies or having a taxation policy that disenfranchises the owners.

A socialistic run government, in determining the fairness (equity) of economic outcomes in society, must also necessarily be involved in controlling other non-working aspects of the lives of its citizens (ex. - obesity may not be allowed since individuals with obesity will need much more health care than others and the added expense wouldn't be fair to society. Mayor Bloomberg's 2012 proposed ban on larger than 16 oz. soft drink sales in New York follows this thought process. Any risk taking activity from a personal or business standpoint would also likely be frowned upon as a possible failure that would burden society). The combination of the extent of control over the economy and social control determine whether a mild form (little governmental involvement) or an extreme form of socialism is being practiced.

Socialism has been practiced in many countries for both short and long (100 years) periods of time. The forms of socialism practiced have been very moderate (U.S.A) to extreme (Russia and China). Governmental control in Russia and China has been over every aspect of its citizens' lives. And, both these systems had been economic and social failures for over 50 years. The socialists of the Democratic party in America today don't want their socialistic agenda to be tainted by the socialistic failures of these two countries, so they describe their form of socialism as different. Their Democratic Socialism is one in which the 'people' control the government vs. the autocrats (Russia and China).

The Democratic politicians, just like most politicians, want to camouflage their true agenda. So, they label their initiatives with words that are palatable to the voting public. Democratic Socialism seems to infer that the voter is somehow in control of the rules and regulations that will emanate from the country voting for a socialistic system. However, millenniums of history confirm that a true democracy (where individuals aren't constrained by excessive governmental control) is so fragile that once any significant power is given to the politicians (a person making his livelihood by lobbying for money and power), it will never return to those who relinquished it. Recent Democratic Socialism is in force in Cuba and Venezuela. The citizens in Cuba revolted for a socialistic platform. And, in Venezuela they voted for it. The citizens of both countries are seriously poor and repressed. And, they also want the thumb of the socialistic government removed from their backs. However, those governments refuse to do so.

Socialism is socialism no matter how it is labelled. In socialistic systems, the government controls to some degree the business community, the wealth it produces, and how that wealth is distributed. Theoretically, the socialistic country's wealth will be distributed somewhat equally so that the gap between the rich and the poor can be justified by society as fair. Even in theory, the definition of fair is completely vague. One would think that those purposing a socialistic system would define the maximum spread (the actual monetary difference of wealth or income between the rich and the poor). Yet, close to 180 years after Karl Marx introduced his theory of socialism, a precise definition of fairness still evades those who advocate for a socialist system. If fairness can't be defined in theory, then how can a system that relies on the concept of fairness exist in the real world?

Ignoring a precise definition of fairness, socialism is pushed by the politicians as being fair anyway. Since aggressive socialistic doctrine actually practiced in many countries has always led to systematic economic failure, the American Democratic party insists that it is the leadership of current and past socialistic countries that was responsible for the poor performance, not the ideology. These leaders falsely claim that democratic elections in America will change the outcome of socialistic policies from terrible to good by preventing corrupt leaders from coming to power.

CHAPTER 1

The fairness concept of equal wealth

T he fairness 'concept' of socialism has been and is very attractive to the thinking of a good portion of the population. And, many types of socialism, from total control by the government of society to determine all citizen's share of wealth (communism) to lesser degrees of control by government (some degree of private wealth, income, and private sector autonomy), have been practiced since the concept was introduced by Karl Marx in the mid-1800s.

The most extreme socialist system (communism) was a total disaster for countries like Russia (1917-1989) and China (1949-1997). Millions of citizens of these countries died from oppression by the masters (heads of the communist party - Lenin, Stalin, etc. of Russia and Mao Tse-tung of China) of the government who grasped power with an iron fist to suppress opposition. Extreme poverty was the standard of living of most of the population of both countries with massive shortages of food supplies and other essential products. Also, the upper bureaucracy of the communistic party lived much better than the masses, so these systems could hardly be considered fair. Initially, the ideology of fairness motivated the general population to go along with moving these countries to socialism. However, once the devastating results showed that these countries' citizens had gone down the wrong path, the people in power and their bureaucracy held too powerful a grip on governmental power to allow a change in political direction, regardless of the majority of citizens wanting change.

Practiced communism in Russia and China redistributed wealth (land, real estate and other valuable assets were confiscated by the government) and created an income system of mostly equal distribution. The wealth disparity between the rich and poor evaporated almost overnight. And, there was no mechanism for an individual to significantly rise up above the masses in terms of wealth, except for the corrupt elite politicians and bureaucrats. In the late 20th century after years of economic failure, both Russia and China were forced to adopt a system that created incentives for individuals to produce more. And, guess who became the wealthy tycoons in both systems. Elite members of the old and newly reformed political system took advantage of the power they had inherited to skim the cream off of the enhanced production of the new order. Putin, the current head of the Russian communist party is a multi-billionaire. And, Xi Jinping, head of the Chinese communist party is also a multi-billionaire. So much for fairness.

Other degrees of socialism have been practiced in other countries. These countries practiced a form of socialism that wasn't total control of business, wealth, and incomes. The main target of these governments was income distribution and redistribution of inherited wealth, not total confiscation. High tax rates on incomes and estates was the method to be used to equalize economic opportunity and wealth. Democratic socialists point to Scandinavia as the model for their ideology. In Scandinavia, elements of the socialistic concept of sharing had been in practice over 100 years. However, in 2004, Sweden eliminated its inheritance tax. And, the other Scandinavian countries except Denmark have also eliminated the inheritance tax. The inheritance tax repudiation wasn't because there was no longer a large gap between the rich and the poor. The tax failed to work as intended. And, it drove wealth overseas and into other tax shelters. The rich didn't get poorer but the middle class did. This added burden on the middle class along with the unintended negative productivity consequences of this tax caused it to be rejected by the Swedes initially and then by other Scandinavian countries. (In 2004, Sweden's political system moved away from hard socialistic policies to a more capitalistic system. And, Sweden, the standard bearer of socialism referenced by the American Democratic party today, now ranks 19th in economic freedom out of 180 countries (U.S.A. ranks 12th)). It has high taxes but also encourages entrepreneurship in spite of the disparity in income and wealth it causes.

The wealth inequality in Scandinavia, after decades if not a century of socialistic policies, is still close to that of the United States (top 10% in U.S. own 76% vs. 66% in Scandinavia). The Scandinavians do pay higher income taxes (top marginal rates of 60.4 - Denmark - 56.9) except for Norway (39%). This isn't that much higher than the U.S. marginal tax rate of 46.3%. The Scandinavian countries tax a very much higher percentage of their population at these high rates. This fact is contrary to the rhetoric of American politicians who say only the rich will have to sacrifice for the benefit of the rest of society. In Scandinavia, it isn't the rich who pay for most of the welfare to the poorer class, it is the middle and upper-middle class or much of the population.

If the goal of a socialistic policy is to more closely equalize wealth distribution, it failed in Scandinavia. If the government can't confiscate wealth from the rich through inheritance tax or an exorbitant income tax because of the economic turmoil such taxes would create, then as in the Scandinavian countries, the poor will be subsidized by the middle and upper middle class with high marginal taxes. Unfortunately, high marginal taxes restrict the mobility of individuals moving from one economic class to another. And, high rates also reduce the incentives of entrepreneurs to start new businesses. According to one study, the share of the richest Swedes who inherited their wealth is around 2/3 with 1/3 being newly rich entrepreneurs. While in the United States, it is the opposite, with 1/3 of the wealthiest inheriting their wealth while around 2/3 are newly rich entrepreneurs. One socialist goal is to create equal opportunity for all those in society. However, it appears that the Scandinavian socialistic policy does much less than the American system in providing that opportunity. The Scandinavian practice of socialism has failed to equalize wealth while also failing to provide as much opportunity for economic mobility and new businesses as the American system.

The Karl Marx doctrine of socialism (really communism) is appealing to many because it appears to rectify the perceived unfairness of a small percentage of the population having so much more than the rest of the population. In the mid-1800s, workers living in severe poverty (little food, horrible housing, no protection from any adverse event that could lead to total deprivation, etc.) was grossly unfair to them (just as it had been since civilization first started). They represented much of the population. And, a redistribution of incomes and wealth presented a solution that would right that wrong. However, in the Western world today, the conditions of the 1800's don't exist. No one dies of starvation in the Western world today. And, shelter and healthcare are also available to the extremely poor. The incentive to become wealthy was available in capitalistic systems the last 200 years. And, the productivity gains achieved by this system massively raised the standard of living of the Western world, so that real poverty (dying of disease and starvation, having no shelter, etc.) no longer exists.

So, should the discussion point being addressed be the one about the 'fairness' of a huge divide in wealth between the rich and the poor, or should it be what economic system is most beneficial to the poor as well as society in general? The evidence, from the last 170 years when comparing economic systems, clearly shows that capitalism's benefit to the world's standard of living so far outpaces any other previous or current economic system, that the difference can be compared to night and day. And, the extreme policies of socialism (communism) have been a total disaster.

Capitalistic policies, not wealth equality policies, created a massive growth in mankind's standard of living. And, all classes of society tremendously benefited. Even though the measuring stick of wealth equality (the percentage ownership of society's assets) shows an increasing wealth divide, the poor have benefited the most from capitalism the last 170 years. Poverty 200 years ago was a daily life and death struggle for the poor. Today, the poor (in the western world) have a social safety net that takes care of them. The rich of 200 years ago could consume all that was available. Today, they have more goods and services to choose from (except for slavery and indenture). Moving away from life and death situations certainly provides a greater increase in the standard of living than having more goods available to consume.

Leading members of the Democratic party today can't deny our country's capitalistic run economy has been hugely economically beneficial, not only to all Americans, but to the rest of the world. However, acknowledging the accomplishments of capitalism would render their socialistic ideology as inferior. So, they focus their arguments for socialism on a myriad of other issues including the equality of outcomes and the equality of everyone in society.

CHAPTER 2

Exceptionalism vs. Egalitarianism
The opposite driving forces of
Capitalism and Socialism

The economy in a capitalistic social environment is driven by the smartest and hardest working members of that society. And, this group of individuals is not static over time as new talent and harder working individuals overtake old talent and older workers. A true capitalistic society is in constant flux as one group of upstarts tries to overtake the old elite group (The richest man in the world today is Jeff Bezos. He was born to a middle class family. Oprah Winfrey was born to a very poor family subject to racial discrimination. Both of these individuals are members of the newly rich that represent 2/3 of the wealthiest Americans.). Capitalism generates economic competition to produce the best product at the lowest price. New ideas augment or replace old ideas in an attempt to unseat older products from the marketplace. And, the old rich are replaced by the newly rich as society benefits from new methods of increasing production being put in place.

Capitalism is an unforgiving system for both entrepreneurs, who try to supplant the old way of doing business, and businesses unable or unwilling to change their method of business. The carcasses of the elite businesses of fifty years ago such as Eastman Kodak, Polaroid, Lehman Brothers, WorldCom, Chrysler, J.C. Penney, etc. have littered the bankruptcy courts.

And, many more have lost 90% of their value from yesteryear. Smaller businesses like car dealerships, video rentals, mom and pop retail and hardware stores along with soda fountains, drive-in movies, etc. have also gone under, destroying what once were successful entrepreneurs. Yet, all these failures have not deterred new entrepreneurs in both small business and big businesses from entering the fray. Most individuals with big dreams (becoming wealthy, extremely wealthy, being your own boss, or showing the world a better mouse-trap, etc.) are willing to take on serious risk (losing all your savings, becoming homeless, divorce, community ridicule, etc.). But, in order to do so, these types of individuals have needed the incentive offered by a system in which their dreams can succeed, regardless of the odds against success. The socialistic system of egalitarianism doesn't offer the rewards necessary to influence these entrepreneurs into following their dreams. The capitalistic system is the only economic system that allows the possibility of making a dream come true. Those that succeed against the serious odds against them are exceptional individuals.

Socialism is an economic system that caters to the status quo and the average individual or the non-risk taker. The socialist wants economic and social equality for all members of its society. As that is the stated goal of socialism, economic equality can be defined as an average well-being for all, with individual outliers of equality being within a narrow range of the average. There is no socialistic manifesto defining the acceptable range above average. However, it is clear that socialists believe the lower range must be close to average (Some of the basic services espoused by socialists are universal health care, education and higher education with health care and educational services being of the same quality that the rich receive. In addition, minimum wages are demanded. But, they are not specifically defined. And socialists believe individuals deserve a choice of where to live, including in the most expensive cities, etc.). In addition, socialists believe that capitalism makes individuals too rich. Too rich is the cap on incomes and wealth allowable under socialism. Socialists espouse that excess incomes or profits are the result of exploitation of the working class, not risk taking that challenges old methods of production to prove that new methods are more productive. As mentioned in the previous paragraph, fortunes have been made and lost by entrepreneurial risk takers. The socialistic narrative that capitalistic individuals make their fortunes off the backs of the working class and for no other reason totally ignores 170 years of economic evidence.

To really understand why a highly socialistic system means disaster for an economy, an individual only needs to understand how egalitarianism undercuts an economy by reducing its citizens' incentive to undertake risk and to work longer hours.

A ridiculous assumption that socialists make is that economic production will not be affected by a change in the incentive structure in the economy due to their policies. By raising taxes and using that 'expected' extra government money to transfer to the poor, the socialists argues that a more egalitarian income system will exist. However, they make a false assumption that society's production will not suffer. The socialist ignores the impact on the economy of their incomes redistribution policy because if production drops significantly, although incomes may become more uniform, the production drop off may mean that the poor end up with less income than prior to redistribution. And, everyone in a society producing less, especially the poor, will suffer (The introduction of socialism in Cuba, Venezuela, Russia, and China resulted in precisely that condition).

Basic economics tells us that supply and demand are related to prices associated with goods and services. Labor is a multi-faceted service. So, the price of labor varies for the service required. High skill jobs pay a lot more than low skill jobs. The high pay encourages workers to earn (through education) the skills necessary to compete for these jobs. As taxation is a negative part of net income, an increasing income tax will reduce job income. And, therefore reduce the incentive for workers to seek high skill jobs. High skill jobs are mostly associated with new industries. These new industries are responsible for the new and better products that increase the standard of living. A policy of income taxation that reduces the labor supply to these industries will repress the growth of them. And, if the increased taxation is severe, as in the socialistic policy of egalitarianism, it is likely that growth of new industries will disappear from a lack of workers.

The distortion to the economics of the labor market by socialistic policies is one of the reasons the economies of all highly socialistic countries fail. The other reason is that income egalitarianism also effects society's investment decisions. In order to control income equality, income earned from investment also has to be controlled. Since 20% of Americans own 86% of the wealth in the country, these individuals' incomes significantly benefit from the incomes they receive from this ownership. Egalitarianism will necessitate that the combined income, from wages and investment income, become more equal in society. Therefore, either investment income will need to be taxed at a very high rate, or the government will need to confiscate a large portion of it. If the government follows either of these policies, future investment opportunities will necessarily be effected negatively.

The top 20% of wealth holders in America are and have been the smartest and hardest working Americans. A socialist policy of severely confiscating their wealth and incomes would disenfranchise these individuals from believing in America. The consequences of an attempt at true egalitarianism would result in these individuals fleeing the county and moving their skill and wealth with them (Why wouldn't these individuals try to protect their assets and standard of living - history shows that they always have. In the Scandinavian countries, the Democrat's model countries of socialism, this was precisely what happened). This country would suffer major economic dislocations that would cause a depression. If government policy was not to redress old income distributions but only future ones, the consequences would still be severe. A policy to restrict the amount of income earned from investments would result in less investment risk-taking. And, this would stop investments going into new industries. And, new investment in general would be severely affected.

Socialists always talk about the rich corporations making too much money. But, this rhetoric also includes the presumption that investors in those rich corporations are also making too much money. Socialists never talk about the corporations that fail or the shareholders that lost their investment money in failed corporations. The reason a discussion about risk and reward never takes place in a socialistic narrative is that egalitarianism has no place for it. The concept of risk and reward cannot be reconciled with the idea. In egalitarianism, there are no winners and losers. Everyone is entitled to the same outcome regardless of their positive or negative contribution to society.

In the real world, every individual understands the concept of risk and reward. Almost every decision made by children and adults is heavily influenced by decisions concerning risk and reward. So, it is hard to believe that socialist give almost no relevance to this in their ideology. Here are just a few examples. 1. Go to school to study to become an expert or go to school to socialize with your friends. Studying requires hours away from friends (risk - social ostracism, reward - higher income as an expert). 2. Spend hours on the basketball court to become a professional athlete or spend hours of apprenticeship in the plumbing profession (risk in choosing an athletic career - chance of success is miniscule and failure will likely lead to lower than average future income, reward - millions in income; risk in apprenticeship - less social interaction, reward - good paying occupation). 3. Investing in social media (risk - losing your whole investment by investing in the wrong (that fails) company with hundreds to choose from, reward - making many multiples of your investment). 4. Buying a lottery ticket (risk -almost certain loss of your purchase price, reward - millions of dollars). The outcomes of these everyday decisions made by all of society determines the income structure of society. In order for socialism to work, socialists must change the outcomes to become equal. Doing so is an impossibility without controlling the whole mechanism of how a capitalistic society works. So, socialism requires a massive amount of control of not only income levels, but also of all the decisions made on the path to determine income levels. All risk vs. reward decisions have to be crafted to achieve parity. Parity requires a loss of freedom and exceptionalism. And, it eventually leads to society's demise.

The socialistic utopian idea that everyone is entitled to be equal with everyone else flies in the face of reality. Also, its idea that all society's citizens should share somewhat equally in society's wealth does not and cannot identify any theoretical or empirical evidence or rationale that can be used to justify the idea. Socialists argue that the discrepancies of wealth in the world are mainly due to the differences in opportunities (education, social ties or relationships, nepotism, etc.) available to different social classes. They claim that this unfairness has to be rectified by reparations from the rich to the poor. Although it is true that class (rich, middle class, poor, etc.) plays a substantial role in determining the future economic status of children, and therefore has been responsible for the average persons' current economic status in America (as in the world), this is not the case for exceptional individuals with the work ethic and the skill set demanded by American industry. The wealthiest American families today are substantially different from those of fifty or one hundred years ago. Originally poor and middle class Americans with exceptional intelligence have moved to the top of the social and economic ladder in America. And, those individuals with an exceptional work ethic have also moved up the ladder. So, while many individuals (13% of the population is considered poor) haven't broken the chain of a poor family, the rest of society seems to be doing just fine. It may be unfair that 13% of the population has to work much harder to break the bonds of poverty, but using a system of egalitarianism doesn't make sense. Reducing the incentives that have increased overall wealth in America will result in a serious reduction in production. Everyone will suffer because of the error of ideological thinking. Exceptionalism and risk taking are the core of capitalism. Poverty is a problem for society, but the solution is not in a socialistic system of egalitarianism.

American government has created all sorts of government programs to help the poor since the 1930s. Government expenditures on socialistic and welfare programs have gone from close to 0% to over 25% of the American GDP in an attempt to better the lives of the less well to do (government spending represents over 35% of GDP today and social programs account for 75% of this spending). One would think that a country spending 25% of its GDP on social programs would alleviate poverty in that country, especially if it was a rich country.

To a certain extent, these government policies did work. The poor today live in much better conditions than the poor did in the 1930s, when the first socialized government programs were enacted. However, spending programs of 25% of the GDP should have resulted in eliminating almost all poverty. Why didn't that happen?

Poverty exists because it is defined as how much the poor can buy (from income received) relative to the purchasing power (income received) of the average American. The ratio of incomes that defines poverty does not consider a change in the poor's standard of living over time. So, the poor today even though enjoying the middle class standard of living of the 1930s are still considered to be living in poverty. The economic bar of poverty has been substantially raised. And, likely it would have been raised more if government programs had incentive features as part of those programs, instead of being mainly socialistic hand-outs. The capitalistic system of incentives created enough wealth in the last 90 years to not only afford paying an additional 25% of the wealth generated to help the poor, but also to massively raise all Americans' standard of living.

Exceptionalism has triumphed in America. Egalitarianism has failed wherever it was tried in the rest of the world. Egalitarianism is a flawed concept. What else is wrong with socialism?

CHAPTER 3

The theoretical foundation of Socialism – The fundamental flaws

T here are many flaws in the underlying assumptions required by the theory of socialism. The most important of them are as follows:

ASSUMPTION 1
Somewhat equal economic sharing is an acceptable practice to most of the population.

While it is generally accepted that equal pay should be the norm for equal work, only a miniscule part of the population believes that any and all work should earn the same paycheck. Difficulty of work, number of hours worked, and quality of work currently accounts for the difference in paychecks. And, there is no public outcry for equal pay checks. The workplace is however filled with complaints of being overworked or underpaid. This fact implies that an analysis takes place to evaluate the competition's work value as reflected in a pay comparison. It also implies that individuals don't want equal pay sharing for different work.

Even if the ridiculous assumption is made that all jobs are equal, and therefore all paychecks should be equal, the socialist theory of equal sharing still has a problem. This has to do with the spending, savings, and borrowing habits of all citizens. The savings and consumption of individuals, in a free society, are the two key elements that determine economic investment. And, therefore the growth of the economy. If a socialistic regime allowed individuals to decide what percentage of their income to spend or invest, then an unwanted future wealth disparity would occur. Those saving a higher portion of income would end up with much more than those saving at the lower rate. The greater the discrepancy in the savings rate, the bigger the discrepancy in future incomes and wealth. In order to avoid future incomes and wealth discrepancies caused by a difference in the savings rate of individuals, socialism proposes that a government central planning commission determines the savings rate of the economy. Individual savings and borrowing would therefore not be allowed to exist. Instead, a certain portion of economic output would be reserved for government investment. And, everyone would be expected to spend their entire yearly income and have no debt. The freedom to make any financial decisions is taken away from millions of consumers and put into a few government hands. Measures to insure income and wealth equality have severe consequences, not only to the rich but also to the rest of society. The control of every aspect of finance in the economy is another freedom grabbing device of socialism.

ASSUMPTION 2

An individual's contribution to society should not be closely correlated to the goods and services society provides the individual.

"From each according to their ability, to each according to their need" is a saying used by socialists to reflect the socialistic philosophy on how goods and services should be distributed to members of the socialistic system. The fundamental flaw of this premise is it trashes economic theory! There is no pricing mechanism for either goods and services or for labor. Goods and services will be supplied whenever they are wanted, and labor will be contributed on an at-will basis as its need is perceived by the worker. There is no incentive to work as the rewards for work are not correlated to the product of the work. How can this socialistic premise be believed by anyone (including the socialists making the argument) living a normal life? From birth, every aspect of life is influenced by a set of incentives to help promote a certain outcome. The materialistic incentive starts with schooling. Children are encouraged to educate themselves in order to get a good future job. Everyone, including socialistic parents, want their children to go to Ivy League colleges so that their children will likely have higher paying future jobs. The reason for having to reward children to affect their behavior implies that the child's natural behavior would have led to a different outcome. And, this is no different than the reward system offered by the economy to adults. Every country in the world has jails, lazy uncles, and nice places to live for a reason. People have extremely diverse interests. And, working isn't usually the priority. So, believing that every individual will do their fair share is an assumption for fairy tales, not reality.

ASSUMPTION 3

The average individual has been responsible for the massive increase in industrial production in the last 200 years.

"If you've got a business, you didn't build that" is a phrase used by President Obama in the 2012 presidential campaign. This phrase represents the thinking of socialists who also claim that capitalistic profits are made of the backs of the worker. For most of history, manpower was almost solely responsible for everything produced in the world. And, the rich and powerful controlled this work force and its production. So, the socialist's assumption was right for most of history. However, with the invention of the steam engine and electricity in the past 200 years, the assumption is now wrong. The massive increases in man's productivity in recent history is attributed to the development of the steam engine and electric power and other associated inventions. Inventions that replaced the labor of man with the labor of the machine have caused the massive increases in production. And, invention is not in the wheelhouse of the average intellect. Only a miniscule portion of the population are inventors. The implementation of inventions into production also isn't in the skill set of the average individual. The genius of a successful entrepreneur is required to get ideas into successful production. Considering that only a tiny portion of the population has been responsible for all the successful inventions of the last 200 years, it is an outrageous claim that the average individual deserves responsibility for the economic successes of the past two centuries.

ASSUMPTION 4

The incentive of making more money than your neighbor isn't a necessary incentive for economic growth.

Since civilization began, man has utilized incentives to influence the actions of other men. The strongest of these incentives is power, status, access to worldly goods, and sex. Money, earned from income or investment, provides the grease that enables individuals to achieve their materialistic goals. It also provides a method to gain power as individuals with excess wealth often become employers. They gain access to political power through campaign and other types of monetary donations and gifts. Money also can finance the production of propaganda, either personal, political, or concerning social and political issues. Money allows individuals to gain status by influencing the perception of the public. The persona, that can be created by money, also is likely to be useful to attract those of the opposite sex. One of the most useful inventions by man is the creation of money. And, since money has been necessary for civilization to operate more efficiently (as a medium of value in every aspect of society - work, property, and services), the benefits money has produced far out-weighs any negatives socialists attribute to it. As man is the most advanced species in the animal kingdom, and money has played an important role in man's development, it can't be logically argued that using money, as an incentive to advance humankind, could be replaced by some other incentive system. Every individual wants at least a little more out of life. Earning more money provides the mechanism to achieve that purpose.

These four assumptions concern the nature of man. The socialistic theory assumes that man is a sharing, non-jealous, non-vindictive, all giving creature. The fact that the opposite is true makes socialistic theory unworkable. And, that is precisely what the historic failure of socialism reveals.

If man was truly as good as the socialistic doctrine requires, equal sharing would be a normal practice, and the huge wealth discrepancies found throughout the world wouldn't exist. But instead of acquiescing to the truth about mankind, socialist claim that there is a small corrupt outlier element in the population. And, these individuals have usurped unfair political and economic power to prevent the natural practice of common sharing. They are the rich!

Somehow for 10,000 years, society has been ruled by the rich elite (even tribal people that live in a subsistence level environment have elite members of the tribe who don't share equally with other members). It is amazing that such a small percentage of the population (the rich) gained so much power in every society since civilization began. How could it be that the majority of citizens have always allowed a corrupt leadership that wasn't interested in equal sharing (the supposed natural nature of man)?! Socialists suggest that the population can now finally throw the corrupt rich under the bus. 10,000 years of history suggests one corrupt ruling class will replace another. It is a quite obvious conclusion from the data, that there always will be a corrupt (very wealthy) ruling class. And, it will always look after its own interests before those of society's.

Socialists claim that by giving all the power to the politicians, society will be better off in America, because the corrupt capitalists will no longer have it. In capitalism, there are many companies always competing for power. In socialism, there is only one huge government. Therefore, the concentration of power in socialism is many degrees higher, as it is almost monolithic. Instead of many corrupt capitalists fighting for power, one corrupt socialistic political party will have all the power. As monopolies are extremely bad for the economy, monopolistic political power is many times worse. The population has the power to corral corporate monopolies, as they did in the early 1900s. However, the population has very little power to fight a monopolistic government. The extreme sacrifice of revolution has been required throughout history. Political dictatorships don't give up power without a fight! Socialism is governmental control of as much as possible. Its goal is monolithic power.

Democrats are talking about the government taking over the job of managing health care, managing energy, managing the educational system, and managing social behavior (political and social correctness) as their lead into managing the whole shebang. And, they want to take most revolutionary power away from the people by confiscating their weapons. They claim the governmental police force will take care of you in your hour of need!

The corrupt elite want to increase their power. Take a lesson from history and don't listen to these expert con artists. The following is a rebuttal of some other of the socialist's favorite arguments.

ARGUMENT 1
Socialistic Fairness and Sharing Concepts

The most basic premise underlying the philosophy of socialism is that any large inequality of ownership or unequal consumption of goods by individuals in society is wrong and unfair. Socialists claim this unfairness is the major reason for the strife and unhappiness in society. In socialism, fair is mainly defined as having distribution of somewhat equal shares of production and wealth regardless of contribution. This type of fairness doesn't exist in nature. The weak and uncommon members of the animal world are either killed by or cast out of the animal group. The strongest and smartest get the 'lions' share of food and their choice of a mate or mates. There is no equality of sharing! And, those who can't produce die. And, in man, the same self-interested behavior and lack of caring for the underachiever has been dominant in all societies.

Mankind has produced nothing but a history of prejudice, slavery, conquest, and power and wealth for the elite (smartest and strongest members of society). The common man throughout history has taken his subordinate place below his leaders accepting the behavior of allegiance and subordination required of him. He expected to get what his rank deserved, less than those above him but more than those below. Fairness was getting what your rank commanded. In most of these societies, rank was mostly determined at birth by family status. In a very few societies, individual merit was highly valued in determining an individual's rank in society. Even in those few societies (Greeks, American Indian, etc.) which allowed individual merit to determine rank, there was never a belief that the members of all ranks of those societies should share either power or wealth equally.

The socialistic concept that wealth should be shared equally runs counter to the natural world's behavior. The implementation of such a concept must therefore be doomed to failure. Also, fairness as defined by the socialist doesn't exist in nature or human behavior. This artificial socialistic solution to creating happiness in mankind, if conscripted by law, therefore would also have to fail.

The question of why a society of equal sharing (or almost equally) sharing has never existed in large societies until 1917 should be asked of the liberal educators, liberal media, and liberal politicians. If this type of society worked best for its participants, why in the 10,000 years of civilization did it rarely exist? And, why after being tried in Russia, China, Eastern Europe, and Cuba for close to 80 years, was it such a failure?

Socialists have long argued that a system that strives for equality in wealth and power is the 'fairest of political systems'. Conjecture and idealistic thinking are not solutions in the real world. Putting bread on the table is. And, apparently for 10,000-years people thought the system of rank was a better system of putting food on the table than socialism. In the last 80 years, after the socialistic idealistic system was put in place, our ancestry was proved correct! Communism in Russia, the most radical form of socialism failed in 1989. Communism in China failed a few years later. These two massive, extensive, and lengthy programs, to test the socialistic theory of wealth sharing, produced massive decay not a vibrant society.

However, this evidence has been ignored as the propaganda machine of the media, educators, and left-wing politicians continues unabated. There has been no acknowledgement of the error in their thinking. Instead, the success of the capitalistic entrepreneur in creating enormous increases in productivity has simply been seen as causing a widening gap between the rich and the poor! The fact that the standard of living of the poor has dramatically increased hasn't been seen as important as the widening of the wealth gap. History has shown capitalism to be superior to socialism in bettering the human condition. The lies promoted by socialistic thinkers that government is good for society has and continues to further the implementation of an inferior system, that history shows will fail.

ARGUMENT 2

All men are created equal and therefore deserve an equal share of the goodies.

Socialism vs. Evolution

God created an infinite diversity of characteristics in man and an equal diversity in the abilities to harness those characteristics. In society, the honing of those characteristics created the civilized world we live in. Characteristics that fulfilled the demands of society were selected, while those that didn't were discarded. The selection process resulted in those individuals with the desired skills being rewarded while those that didn't meet the standard were cast aside.

Unfortunately, God didn't create only individuals with the desired skill set! Let's label the group with the desired skill set achievers, and the group without it the non-achievers. Achievers produce what society wants while non-achievers don't. Also, as part of God's basket of characteristics, self-interest and self-gratification were also included.

In order for society to obtain the most out of the achievers, it must provide the most gratifying rewards for the self-interested achiever. Money, wealth, and power (sex also) have been the historic reward system for man. And, as man is the most successful of all the animal species, this reward system's merits can't be contested as a poor system. The socialistic goal of income and wealth equality is completely lacking in similar rewards. The nebulous reward of a 'fair' society for those inspired by socialism is totally contrary to the reward system based on self-interest, which has provided so much progress for mankind.

The joy of sharing doesn't cut it as a replacement for the self-interested reward system that society evolved for man. All highly socialistic societies are underachievers in fulfilling their citizens' needs because they have failed to produce a better reward system which doesn't include power, money and wealth. The failure to provide the right incentives for the achievers in Russia, China, Cuba, and other communist countries resulted in poverty for its citizens. Also, aristocracies or other government forms that only provided incentives for the elite greatly lagged in the economic development of their economies. The economies in Latin American and South Asian countries are prime examples, as their standards of living are extremely lower than those of the Western World.

Note also that not only does the better reward system produce more goods for its citizens, but in doing so also creates a more compassionate atmosphere for the non-achiever. Successful societies produce a surplus of goods. The greater the surplus, the less reason there is to hoard those goods. Rich societies are therefore more tolerant. Also, the well-to-do citizens of these societies are willing to provide a higher standard of living for the non-achievers than in poor societies. Maslow's hierarchy of human needs provides the reason for this as wealthy individuals seek to fulfill spiritual needs, and therefore view the poor in a better light. By replacing a successful reward system with the introduction of a failed reward system, those who advocate for extreme wealth sharing are dooming the non-achiever to the worst possible outcome, a lower standard of living and a less compassionate society.

In early times when societies were poor, the most unproductive became beggars. And, if they were lacking in begging skills, they died. Today in the developed countries, it is thought that nobody is worthless enough to let die. And, it is also thought that compassion helps a society become more cohesive. Wealthy societies with excess production have chosen to support the non-achievers with this view, as the rewards from the karma of giving outweighs the diminished importance of having excess surplus. However, as the surplus owned by the achievers diminishes, they are much less inclined to give it away. As the measure of society's wealth decreases, the value of karma from giving also decreases, which results in less giving.

If a society controlled by achievers changes to one controlled by non-achievers, production will decline as non-achievers will attempt to use their power to increase the percentage of their rewards from production. As achievers anticipate the rewards from their labor (and investment) will decline, this disincentive will cause the achiever to readjust his personal priorities away from production. All attempts to make achievers conform to giveaways to the government through taxes or through regulations (minimum wage laws, healthcare benefits, etc.) will cause society's production to decline as achievers chose gratifying non-productive efforts to replace those of production. This is not a hard concept to understand as every aspect of society from family to the work environment uses incentive to motivate the individual. And, as incentives decrease, behavior attributed to those incentives is less influenced and vice-versa.

It's amazing that liberal educators and liberal media ignore or minimize the concept of incentive as a driving force for economic production, especially when their own personal lives revolve so much around this concept!!! In addition, socialists never acknowledge the huge differential in the production capabilities of the productive members of society vs. the non-productive members of society. This differential is due to God's gift to man in the form of diversity. Turning a blind eye to the truth, educators and the media still proclaim the virtues of socialism. This irresponsible behavior has resulted in voters believing in a failed unnatural system. America could be on the brink of completing the process of implementing socialism as its political system, thanks to some very incompetent intellectuals who hold sway over the public!

The War of Independence must be fought again. The aristocratic monarchy isn't the enemy this time, but the political juggernaut of socialism is. And, the Democratic Party is at its head! True Americans need to join the battle to convince the public that the bag of goodies being offered by the liberals is the same bag offered by con-artists. There is nothing but rocks inside.

ARGUMENT 3

The goodness of sharing and fellowship will make the world a better place.

Darwinian Theory at Odds with Socialism

Most liberals believe the implementation of liberal ideas can make the world a better place. A significant concept associated with liberal ideas is that many citizens of the world are treated unfairly. And, laws need to be instituted to make the world a fairer place. In the liberal's mind, although most discussion concerns economic welfare, the closer everyone is to having the same worldly goods, and the same physical and mental attributes, the closer mankind would be to nirvana. When everyone is equal, how can unfairness exist?

A case might be made for clones but that argument ignores the Darwinian theory of survival of the fittest. In Darwinian theory, diversity in a species is essential for the survival of that species. So, if ultimate fairness is the prime objective of liberal policy, then if achieved the results may lead to extinction. Luckily, God created man with many different physical and mental attributes. Thus, allowing him to adapt to his environment and survive.

Unfortunately, man's diversification necessarily created the unfairness liberals are trying to rectify. History is the record of man taking for himself or his companions as much as possible, with total disregard to fairness toward other fellow men. Unfair advantage determined the winners and losers. As man is the dominant and most successful animal species in the world, does it make sense to promote a policy to change man's use of unfair advantage? The 'survival of the fittest theory' suggests that inferior members of a species die, leaving only the strongest to live and breed. Is this unfair? If so, shouldn't Mother Nature or God who created the inferior be blamed?

The conflict among men trying to use their unfair advantage has been the impetus that has driven societal and economic development. Almost everyone in the developed world lives better than the aristocracy of the 19th century. If the present concept of liberal fairness was prevalent in historic times, our species may not exist today and the western world's standard of living certainly wouldn't!

ARGUMENT 4
Community Sharing Trumps Self-Interest

An underlying assumption of socialism is that the sharing of production (especially equal sharing despite unequal worker production) is an acceptable practice among most members of society. Without majority acceptance of this socialistic tenant, many detrimental problems with production will occur as individuals attempt to evade sharing rules.

The actual behavior of individuals in society indicate that minimal sharing might be acceptable. However, since most individuals tally a fairness count in every relationship they maintain, the tolerance for unequal sharing is very low. An example of this tally is the calculation of the sum of money spent by each party of a relationship in joint outings (dinners, movies, etc. - birthday or Christmas gifts, etc. are also a subject of calculation), and the corresponding services received to determine if each party paid the appropriate share. The fairness tally for each relationship is a running total that takes into account the generous occasions in which one party pays the bill, but expects reciprocal treatment sometime in the future. A vast majority of relationships fail when reciprocity doesn't occur. And, therefore the 'injured' party feels unfairly treated. Even in America's rich society, a couple of hundred dollars is often enough to destroy friendships! And, what brother or sister happily lends (gives) money to their lazy free-loading siblings?! The saying 'never lend money to family and friends' didn't just come to pass for no reason!

In all societies, the counting behavior is equally prevalent at all levels. Neither the achievers nor the non-achievers want to contribute (share) more than they receive from others. They may be persuaded to share, if confronted by a hostile group (pressure from family members, community or political groups) demanding achievers pay 'their fair share'. However, the achiever will try to mitigate the loss by spending less future time on production, or trying to evade the confiscation in some other manner.

In most societies the hostile group will be the non-achievers or their representatives. And, depending on the extent of the hostility, deference and some sharing (by paying high taxes or making charitable contributions) is prudent! However, since the achiever doesn't want to relinquish a disproportionate share of his production, he will do everything possible to avoid that circumstance (tax evasion and production cuts are very probable outcomes).

In a democratic system, the process (taxation and regulation) causing unwanted sharing is likely to become excessive and detrimental to production, since the non-achievers representing the majority of voters, can exert political power over the achievers. American democracy did not accommodate total rule of the masses through most of it history. Up until 1930, the governmental control over citizens' incomes was modest. And, therefore wealth equality couldn't be dictated by the underachievers, even though they represented the majority of voters. America's Constitution and Bill of Rights had been drafted by men who dreaded governmental interference in their private, public and business affairs. Both achievers and non-achievers were convinced that freedom was better than governmental control. And, the idea of wealth sharing was deemed ridiculous. So, for about 150 years, the democratic process didn't work against the achievers. The Great Depression and the policies of President Franklin Roosevelt changed this.

Times were so bad that the American people turned to a leader who promised to change things for the better. By enacting governmental work programs and other welfare programs, such as free food programs, the suffering of those out of work was mitigated to a certain extent. Although there is debate as to whether these governmental actions were the most appropriate, they achieved a floor for the suffering level of those out of work.

Unfortunately, the American people relinquished a part of their independence in exchange for the government taking care of them. This crack in the American philosophy, to keep government out of people's affairs, has allowed the politicians to pry for even larger cracks in order to cater to America's non-achievers. Dependence on the government was no longer 100% unacceptable in society's mind. The reasons for dependency would grow over time and finally in 1964, President Lyndon Johnson's 'Great Society' made the crack a chasm. He implemented policy based on the premise that non-achievement was the result of a concerted effort by the achievers to maintain the status quo of the non-achiever.

Since then, instead of the government being the enemy of the people, as in the eyes of our forefathers, the achievers became the enemy of the people in the eyes of society. The politicians had moved the country into a position to be controlled by the non-achievers. The democratic process and the fact that non-achievers represent the largest proportion of the populace would assure that outcome.

The process would take time as the majority of the population was doing well, as achievers boosted the economy. The seeds of this new philosophy, however, were sprouting everywhere. Hostile political organizations representing non-achievers were organizing and growing. And, their demands were starting to echo everywhere. Politicians were listening and enacting hundreds of new regulatory laws and new taxation policies.

Coercion of the achievers to share became a bigger part of the law. It had also become a socially accepted brain washing practice. In spite of society's brain washing, achievers never changed to like or want to share. They also never liked the government telling them what they could or couldn't do. They were no different in that respect than the non-achievers.

If hassle and the demand for sharing are moderate, the achiever will continue to produce (although at a modified pace). As the scale of each increases, his production will correspondingly decrease and may even put him in the category of non-achiever. What started out as moderate demands of the non-achiever in the 1960s became more aggressive over the next 50 years. America has reached the stage that with 50% of the population receiving some kind of government payout, many achievers have decided to become non-achievers.

Government dependence programs reduced the incentive to work, and in many cases made it unprofitable to work through 2016. Many achievers became non-achievers. President Trump has instituted policies to seriously reduce regulation and government interference in achiever's lives. And, the economy has turned around. No longer are 11 million people unemployed. The unemployment rate is the lowest since 1969.

However, elite democrats and the Democratic Party continue to push for the achievers to give just a 'little more', or a lot more. The 'little more' disincentive along with massive regulation almost put the U.S. economy into a depression in 2008. It drove achievers to become non-achievers. And, it perpetuated the downward pressure on economic production. In 2008, with over 11 million workers unemployed, and much more underemployed in America, wasn't the policy to accommodate the non-achiever the wrong policy?! Luckily, a pro-achiever president was elected in 2016. And, his policies have led to a massive increase in American wealth.

50+ years of programs to share the wealth, since President Johnson, lead America to the brink of insolvency with the government owing $16 trillion! And, still the cry from the media and educators was the non-achiever was not getting enough! These intellects had forgotten that the achievers' response to an increasingly hostile environment (additional confiscation by the government) would result in the human behavior of shielding against this threat. That's why 50% of the population had moved toward the non-achiever status.

The socialistic concept of fairness, that sharing wealth for the community's benefit will create a harmonious society, is totally unrealistic and unworkable. The socialistic idea, that most people are unselfish and would rather promote more equality by donating a portion of their assets versus being mostly self-interested, has no supporting empirical evidence. By actively advocating this core element of socialism, educators and media have helped move America closer to a socialistic system where the government takes from the achievers to give to the non-achievers. With government controlling 40% of economic spending in the country, the socialistic policies of the last 80 years had strangled the country until 2016.

You liberals, don't you think you should recognize what led to looking over the edge of the economic cliff, before continuing to commit to pushing America over it by insistence on your failed philosophy?!!!

ARGUMENT 5
The Common Good Outweighs Individual Benefits

Socialists argue that capitalism promotes only self-interest whereas socialism promotes the common good. Therefore, socialism is a better system than capitalism.

The idea of common good can easily be characterized as looking out for your neighbor. This idea has existed since the beginning of time, as this practice was done for the 'common good' especially in troubled times. It arose out of neighbors looking out for each other when it was a necessity for survival. Reciprocal sharing, as a part of survival, meant that each party would help the other if needed. And, the favor would be returned in the future. Reciprocal sharing was not a one sided affair of always giving while the other side was always taking. In fact, the thought 'you owe me' was always present in historical times as well as today!

The socialistic philosophy eliminates the 'I owe you' from the concept of sharing. The non-achievers receive benefits from society regardless of a reciprocal contribution. You might say the behavior advocated by the church is the same behavior advocated by socialism - 'giving is as good as receiving' and 'each side gets equal benefit'. Who, among the liberals, practices that act of giving?! In the past, salvation of the average man's soul compelled him to give 10% of his income to the church to help his fellow man. The rich members of the church could have afforded much more. But, it was against their nature to give more, so the church only asked for what they thought they could receive! Giving for the common good when combined with the reward of salvation weren't compelling reasons to share a significant portion of one's wealth in the past!

Self-interest has dominated human behavior since the beginning of time. Isn't it better to be ruled by a system, the capitalistic system, that adheres to natural behavior than to be ruled by one, socialism, that doesn't? Has human nature really changed in the last 50 years to make liberals think they can pass off the idea of substantial 'sharing' as workable, because it is for society's common good. I think not!

ARGUMENT 6

The Answer to Happiness is Wealth Equality not Freedom

Socialist argue that the wealth gap between the 'rich' and the 'poor' is unfair and causes much of the unhappiness in society. They argue that the government must therefore be empowered to rectify this inequity. They believe that the narrower the gap, the happier society will become. This argument presupposes that other factors, either individually or jointly, do not play a larger role in the happiness of society's citizens. Although jealousy (envy of other man's economic status) is the powerful human emotion that can be attributed to the socialist's argument, it is hardly the driving force of human happiness.

Socialists would be well advised to take a course in human psychology to better understand the fallacy of this underpinning assumption in their philosophy. In fact, the United States of America was founded on the premise that freedom and the freedom to pursue happiness without government intervention was the most powerful motivator of human happiness.

The veracity of this premise is that the U.S. has achieved the status of being the most powerful, wealthiest country in the world. And, for well over 200 years, migration to the U.S. has been unstoppable. The 'American Dream' is to build a better life for yourself and your family. And, it has nothing to do with equal distribution of wealth. The fact that millions have come to America in spite of a massive gap between the rich and the poor pokes a huge hole in the argument for wealth equality.

The concept that wealth inequality creates tension in society is true. However, it is the thought process of jealous people that turns wealth inequality into the unfair category. Jealousy is a powerful human characteristic that needs a reason to justify the emotion. The socialistic politician provides that reason with the notion that the rich stole their wealth from the poor (by paying unfairly low wages to accumulate their wealth). This type of politician also criticizes the rich as selfish and uncaring to create an even more powerful negative image of the rich. This is done to further promote jealousy and class warfare.

However, selfishness is a very powerful human characteristic common to all men, not just the rich. The socialist's idea that the world would be a better place if there was more equality and sharing might be true. However, this would require mankind to change its nature. All humans are selfish and jealous (except possibly for saints). And, changing these characteristic of mankind is beyond the scope and capability of government (even if the government was run by saints - the few who aren't selfish and jealous).

The selfishness and jealousy in man is evidenced by observing everyday life, or just taking note of every individual's own behavior. In order to capture followers, socialists must inflame human emotions to promote societal conflict in order to overpower rational thinking. The fact that the socialistic argument for wealth equality requires increasing conflict in society is another negative factor against it.

There are many socialistic talking points exclaiming the virtues of wealth equality. Most people want to achieve perfection in themselves and society. They perceive the perfect world to be one where everyone is happy. They see equality as a necessity for happiness, as comparing status in their current life is a major element of their current happiness or unhappiness. Unfortunately, God did not create a perfect world of equality. Instead, he created a Darwinian world. And, in that world, wealth equality does not lead to the greatest satisfaction of mankind. And, attempts to achieve ideal wealth equality have historically only produced massive suffering. Happiness has been greatest in the American way of life that promotes freedom for the individual to do what he wants.

ARGUMENT 7

Government rule is better than
Capitalistic Rule of the Economy

The current claim, of the liberals and the socialistic Democratic Party today, is that the Government is able to create social and economic policy that is more beneficial to society than the capitalistic system. They believe that a small group of elite politicians is better at understanding the needs of the public than the capitalistic market place, where the interaction of millions of entrepreneurs and customers (determined solely by self-interest) determine individual happiness and also production.

Socialism was first proposed in the 19th century by Karl Marx. He stipulated that the general population would be better off if a socialistic system was put in place to more equally distribute a country's wealth. His theory was put in practice in a number of diverse countries in Europe, Russia, and China. After close to 100 years of these political systems being in place, the for-profit system in the U.S. has provided a standard of living many times higher for the general population than that achieved by those socialistic systems. (The standard of living in Russia is less than 1/5th the standard of living in the U.S. And, the standard of living in China is less than 1/10th the standard of living in the U.S.)

In addition to a higher standard of living, the for-profit system allows for less governmental interference in its citizens' lives. Socialistic systems require a myriad of rules, regulation and enforcement in how goods and services will be redistributed between producers and consumers, in order to insure a semblance of providing the individual with his fair or equal share of production.

Also, risk taking behavior; in business (ex. - developing a new product), in recreation (ex. - extreme sports), in food consumption (enjoying salty and sugary foods that increase the chances of diabetes and heart disease), and in an infinite number of other areas; is likely to result in draining society's resources in the event of business failure, traumatic injury, health issues, and other costly issues. Therefore, the socialistic system must attempt to prevent this type of activity, as it would be unfair for the rest of society to have to subsidize the cost associated with risk taking behavior (In 2012, New York city's Mayor Bloomberg proposed rules to regulate the sale of 32 ounce sodas because the huge sugar intake is unhealthy and likely to lead to diabetes thereby putting a burden on the city's health system).

A capitalistic society does not have the above mentioned burden of regulating peoples' lives in an attempt to maintain the equality of consumption among its citizens. This additional freedom in a capitalistic society adds to the increased sense of well-being in for-profit societies vs. socialistic societies. The concept that a socialistic society is better suited for the happiness of its citizens is false for the reasons cited above.

ARGUMENT 8
Profit Only Serves the Rich

Socialists will make the argument that since Government is a non-profit entity, the transfer of commerce to it from a for-profit entity will result in the same quantity and quality of goods being produced. However, without unearned wealth (profit) being unfairly distributed to the capitalist, more goods would be available to the workers. Therefore, the socialistic argument is that capitalism provides no benefits to society as the government can reproduce (quantity and quality) the goods and services of a capitalistic society, without giving a piece to non-workers.

There are an overwhelming number of examples in America of the fallacy of that argument. The comparison between the services and costs of the U.S. Post Office and that of Federal Express might be one of the best examples. Post Office prices are much higher than those of Federal Express. In addition, the Post Office doesn't offer as many services as Federal Express. This is in spite of the fact that the Post Office had a monopoly on U.S. mail deliveries for over 150 years (And, also the Post Office is operating at a huge loss every year while Federal Express is extremely profitable). In fact, in spite of the private industry's profit margin, every business run by the private sector that competes against government service is much more cost effective.

The difference in the incentive program in private industry is so much greater than in the government that it creates a much more productive work environment, in regard to innovation and hard work (Owners and employees will work harder and create better ways of doing tasks if they are rewarded through higher profits or higher pay). The resulting increase in productivity allows owners to take a share of the production, while still having more product than would be available if run by a non-profit government entity (Government is structured to benefit those who follow the rules, not those who are innovative. Therefore, workers who try to change the system of doing things to increase productivity are not significantly rewarded for success. In fact, in many cases, their fellow workers feel threatened if one individual's productivity increases above the mean, as superiors will question the work ethic of the fellow workers).

Worker incentive is at the heart of the capitalistic system. Worker incentive and wealth equality are diametrically opposed. Worker incentive means direct participation in a share of the wealth the worker creates. Wealth equality means an equal share of the wealth produced by all workers regardless of difference in the amount of contribution. Lazy or unskilled workers receive similar amounts as the more productive. It is quite obvious that incentive drives human behavior. And, therefore the socialist's argument that the distribution of profit reduces the goods available for the worker is totally fallacious. In fact, the profit incentive creates more goods for both the profiteer and the worker.

ARGUMENT 9
A Socialistic Government is Efficient

Another argument against governmental control of wealth distribution concerns the inefficiencies caused by this societal system. The socialistic system requires that distributions be made according to governmental rules, which are enforced by governmental bureaucracies. In the more socialistic countries, larger portions of the country's wealth need to be distributed. This requires a larger governmental bureaucracy, which is needed to run its larger programs of regulation and redistribution. Aside from the lack of employee incentives to create efficient programs, the resources drained away, to support the bureaucracy, from producing tangible economic product make the socialistic system grossly inefficient. So, not only does the practice of wealth equality reduce the achiever's incentive to work, but it also creates more inefficiency by causing resources to be allocated to the non-productive task of administering programs of reallocation instead of programs that increase production.

ARGUMENT 10

Capitalism is more corrupt than Socialism

Socialists believe that a society run by the government is less corrupt than a society run by capitalism. The assumption made by this socialist argument is that the politicians who run the government for the 'benefit' of the public aren't as corrupt as the businessmen who run corporations for only their benefit and that of the owners. This assumption is ludicrous as all people are made from the same mold. Power corrupts regardless of the entity from which it emanates. As government is more powerful than any single business, corruption is greater in government than business. Abuse of power has never been reserved in its application.

In every political or economic structure, self-interest causes those with power to use it to their advantage. (In some cases, what is thought as abuse of power is actually usurpation of power. In any case, when the majority of citizens in a society feel unfairly treated by a power structure, this power structure can be considered abusive.) The larger any organization, (religious, political or economic), the greater is the inherent power of that organization. And, if the organization has a hierarchical leadership structure, then all the power of the organization resides in its small leadership.

The Government is the largest entity in the U.S. The Federal budget is $4.75T while the city, county, and state budgets total around another $3.4T. At the Federal level, 536 individuals, the Senators, the House Representatives, and the President, all have a say in how the budget will be spent. If the budget were divided equally among these members, each would control over $8B in yearly spending decisions. This tremendous power would even tempt the most honest individual to use his influence to better himself. Although there is a litany of rules against abuse of their political positions, somehow all these politicians become multi-millionaires, either while in office or shortly thereafter. Their salaries, as politicians, don't account for their drastic increase in wealth (ex. - President Clinton has earned $100M+ since he left office in 1998. And, President Obama has also earned almost $100M in the 3 years since he left office.)! Could it be that these politicians are as self-interested as the elite businessman?

Corruption is the abuse of power. So, the question as to which system is more corrupt than the other can be addressed by understanding the power structure of each system. In a true Adam Smith capitalistic system, the free market determines the power structure. The entrepreneur has to conform to the free market. Otherwise, he will go out of business. The Adam Smith scenario envisions competition to thwart the accumulation of power. However, in the real world, successful businesses when combined with leveraging politics have resulted in very powerful businesses being created. The power associated with these big businesses has often resulted in corruption.

However, governments have always had more power than any single one business. And, government is a hierarchical structure where the most power is concentrated in the upper echelon. Since socialism's concept relies on government taking care of its citizens in all aspects of their lives, its power structure is many times greater than that of a capitalistic orientated political structure. Therefore, since concentrated power produces the most corruption, it follows that a socialist government is much more corrupt than a capitalistic run government. And, a historical review of government structures reveals that to be the case.

ARGUMENT 11

Capitalists Take Advantage of the Working Man

A socialistic argument often starts with the premise that since maximizing profits is the sole motivation of capitalism, capitalists have no interest in the common well-being of society, which requires attention to other factors (ex.- charity, decent wages, respect for fellow men, etc.). And, socialists argue that the worker is at the mercy of the capitalist. Therefore, capitalism is an anti-social, evil concept. Socialists point to the plight of the worker all through the Industrial Revolution, as well as the gap between the rich and the poor today, to make their point (Protecting workers from the negative effects of low wages and poor working conditions, etc. created by totally self-interested powerful businessmen plays well on the sympathetic ears of the public as workers represent a much larger portion of society than entrepreneurs).

The missing part of the socialistic argument is that a capitalistic society opens opportunity for every member of society. The hard worker and the entrepreneur coming from all types of backgrounds are presented with opportunities to better their lives. Both successful risk taking and the hard work ethic are rewarded with either financial rewards or social advancement or both. Successful risk takers are usually more successful than the hard worker. And, therefore they are the individuals most able to move up society's social ladder to the elite level. In addition, political power can be obtained through the economic influence gained by the risk taker. By promoting hard work and risk taking, the capitalistic society is constantly increasing productivity, social mobility and the standard of living of the people living in that society.

By encouraging new risk taking ideas that lead to more productivity, the power of the human brain is unleashed to create powerful economic growth. Although society benefits greatly with each successful new idea, each corresponding risk taker's benefits are astronomical in comparison to the average individual's increase in wealth due to the new idea (when a new product benefits millions of people, even taking a tiny piece of the total benefit creates huge returns for the entrepreneur). This is a major cause in the disparity of wealth between rich and poor, not stealing from, or taking advantage of, or abusing the worker.

New more productive systems do have short-term negative economic effects. They cause economic displacement. Old jobs are no longer needed. And, workers need to learn new skills to be valuable (worker displacement during the Industrial Revolution led to the rise in the idea of socialism). This period of displacement also widens the wealth gap between the rich and the poor (even if just on a short-term basis). Social unrest occurs as workers lose jobs and also their accustomed standard of living, while the capitalist benefits. This scenario causes socialists to find evil in the capitalistic system (The rich are portrayed as evil because they 'don't care' about the people 'they' put out of work). And, if the disparity of wealth significantly increases over time, the power structure of society will also change.

If the new systems put in place creates a huge increase in productivity, the risk taker's enterprise will grow rapidly and gain huge economic and political power. If left unfettered, this power will at some point become corrupt. Socialists attribute this extreme evil of unfetter power to the capitalistic system. When in fact, the same corruption of power occurs even more often in aristocracies and other political systems (Unfettered capitalism, in the early 1900's, in the new industries of steel and oil led to massive corporations who used their power unfairly. The Sherman Anti-Trust Act was passed to dilute the power of the huge companies engaging in anti-competitive practices).

Instead of following a rational thinking process, that economic progress (more efficient production) naturally will lead to social disruption (through workers put out of work needing to develop new skills), the socialist blames the capitalist for that negative outcome. But, he doesn't credit the entrepreneur for society's overall economic gain (more productive capacity). Although the (distasteful) profit causes the eventual advancement (through increased production) in the well-being of society, socialists will never acknowledge this huge benefit of capitalism.

Successful new technologies often result in the rapid growth of companies, causing the original entrepreneur to lose control of his company to professional business managers. These individuals are many times more interested in milking the new technology for their own benefit, rather than in using the new profits to discover other more productive technologies.

They use the power of the large asset base of the company for propaganda (marketing), negotiations (with workers and suppliers) and political agendas (lobbying) to enhance the company's short-term profitability and their own salaries. Once company control is passed to professional business managers, unless the owners take an active role, those businesses lose much of their capitalistic characteristics. They become replaced with many aspects of crony capitalism (Cronyism is defined as favoritism shown to friends without regard to their qualifications as in helping them gain positions they are unworthy of).

Entrepreneurs seeking long-term profitability require the most efficient systems in order to achieve it. Professional business managers, who don't have an ownership stake in the company except with options, are much less concerned with optimal long-term profitability. In the short-run, the anti-competitive actions described above by professional managers help fend off the competition of newer, more productive ideas. In the long-run, these large companies fail as increasingly productive ideas from smaller entrepreneurial companies take away market share.

Crony capitalism leads to failure. Socialists lump companies with professional businesses managers (crony capitalism) together with true capitalism (entrepreneurial managed businesses) and cite the injustices of crony capitalism to indict the true capitalistic system (A current example is the 2008 housing bubble where professional business managers put in place a massive risk taking process that entrepreneurs would never have initiated. The owners or shareholders of the large banks lost most of their equity while the managers - CEOs, etc., - made millions before the collapse and lost nothing after). The portrayal of crony capitalism as true capitalism is another major error in the socialist's argument about the evils of capitalism.

When one views the history of capitalism in the western world, it has shown that a constantly changing economic and political hierarchy takes place under that system. As huge businesses rise and fall, so does their economic power and political influence. And, although change (caused by better technology) in the business environment causes economic disruptions (recessions and depressions), the benefit of the economic progress (more production by more efficient means) has resulted in social and economic mobility for the working man. It has also resulted in the massive improvement of the standard of living in the western world in the last 200 years. In western society, the poor are living many times better than the aristocracy of the 1800s. The average man has taken advantage of the capitalistic system, not vice-versa.

ARGUMENT 12

Socialism is more productive than Capitalism

Capitalism promotes economic growth by creating a competitive system that encourages individuals to work for a better life, in terms of economic product and health matters. Socialism, on the other hand, does not promote economic growth, but instead promotes the concept of fairness and equality as a way to happiness. This policy necessarily causes economic stagnation, if not economic decay.

Socialists make the presumption that, in general, individuals in society are more concerned with the wealth equality of society than with increasing their own wealth. It follows therefore that if any individual's personal wealth increases at a faster rate than society's, a disequilibrium will occur (the spread between the rich and the poor will increase), causing an unwanted condition in a socialistic society. Then, in order for a socialistic society to increase the general wealth of the society without changing wealth distribution, it would have to require all citizens to work harder as a group or become more productive by improving systems currently in place.

Problems are evident in either case that would and have historically prevented society's economic advancement, in a socialistic system. If one presumes socialistic societies have a mandate from their citizens to increase production, then, in the first case, all working members of the socialistic society would have to agree to commensurately increase their workloads to ensure fairness and the maintenance of the wealth status quo of the system. Otherwise, the increase in the work load would be unevenly distributed, and wealth distribution would change.

Mass acceptance will not occur because the task of getting a majority of people to agree on anything is hard enough, let alone getting everyone to agree to reduce their leisure time without rules to punish those that didn't comply. Voting to sacrifice for the 'common good' only happens in the most dire circumstances. Therefore, it would be impossible for a socialistic society to increase its standard of living by asking all its citizens to work harder.

In the second case, in order to improve systems or productivity requires ingenuity and risk taking (attempting a new untried process). As mentioned before, neither attribute is highly regarded in a socialistic society. The learning by trial and error exposes the socialistic society to a possible loss of wealth. And, there is no gauge to accurately evaluate the likelihood of success or failure. Only new projects that received the consensus of a socialistic committee would have a chance of being funded. And, history shows that successful entrepreneurs build businesses counter to accepted beliefs. Therefore, the culture of socialism will prevent the improvement in productivity because approval of successful new different methods to improve systems will not happen. The underlying assumption that maintenance of wealth equality is essential to happiness in the socialistic system ensures, at best, there is no wealth growth in the purely socialistic system. The historical outcome of socialistic societies is one of not only no growth, but decay.

ARGUMENT 13
Liberal Philosophy results in Positive Community Behavior

Liberals will surely argue that the selfish behavior of the elite in history was deplorable (all wealth was owned by the aristocracy and they provoked wars to rearrange the aristocratic hierarchy). Some liberals attribute the elite's bad behavior to the poor economic environment of the past. However, now that worldly goods are plentiful, they believe it's time for the elite to become more civilized and share their wealth (It is very interesting to note that the sharing the wealth concept is only openly promoted in the developed world, not in the under-developed or developing world).

One would assume, based on the liberal ideology, that mankind is good, generous, and unselfish. Since liberal ideas believe selfishness is bad and sharing and forgiveness are good, one might think that the liberal's value system was a product of their childhood experience, where they experienced sharing and forgiveness and were happy because of it.

These individuals must have grown up in the ideal family, where there was no conflict for attention, resources, or differing ideas, and where the workload of household duties, chores, and bringing in the bucks was shared happily by family members. Also, each member of the family would have had no jealousy about another's looks, intellectual or athletic abilities, or social skills. And, there were no sibling or parental preferences that created ill feelings. In addition to the perfect family setting, it might also be assumed that these liberals must have also grown up in perfect social settings also. If somehow, an unfortunate incident occurred such as being bullied, being criticized, being called a loser in sports, or just running into the wrong person, these liberals would have excused these actions by believing that they were outlier events. And, the people involved could be changed for the better. Although these events would be unpleasant, the liberal would never carry a grudge or seek revenge, even in his mind.

If the liberal mindset is not based on an experience of sharing and forgiveness, but based on a perception that childhood life would have been better if family and acquaintances would have been nicer (because they shared and forgave), then the liberal philosophy is dependent on dreams that utopia can exist, if most people change their behavior. This dependence on the hope that mankind will change its characteristic of selfishness is a far cry from the liberal propaganda that blames only the few rich members of society for being responsible for all that is unfair and wrong. The task of changing the behavior of a few seems within the realm of possibility. The task of changing the behavior of all of mankind would be viewing as an impossible task, even by most liberals. So in order to retain their liberal outlook, these individuals must ignore actual human behavior to fool themselves.

Core elements of the liberal's belief system are as follows. Liberals articulate their belief that love triumphs over hardship. They say they believe that peace triumphs over individual needs for worldly goods. They insinuate that people are more interested in the welfare of those around them than in their own welfare. They publish the belief, that if someone has different values than their own, somehow society is at fault. And, somehow that fault must have been unintentional, since most people in society want the best for each other. They believe that competition in any field should be filled with comradery, without motive to show oneself better or to gain reward.

With this liberal belief system in mind, it would be informative to determine whether the life styles of leading liberals conform to their espoused belief system. The current leading list of liberals includes movie stars, wealthy financiers, wealthy politicians and wealthy business men. And, of course there is Mother Theresa. I would assume that with a common belief system, they would all share equally, and have all lived their lives with as much consideration for those less privileged than themselves.

Take a hard look at the facts. Need I say more? Do liberals lead double lives, one advocating the politics inspired by their idealistic views while the other harshly competing in the real world? If this elite list of liberals care so much about the inequality of means in the world, then why don't they share enough of their wealth, with those in need, to bring about an equal means status for everyone.

As an example, if this elite group, as a whole or individually, thought an income of $200K/year was an appropriate sharing income level, and their level of income was $2M/year, then these individuals should give away $1.8M/year. This amount could then be divided among individuals earning less to supplement their incomes to a level of $200K. So, instead of complaining about inequality, while owning multiple million dollar houses, flying private jets, vacationing at $1000+ per night resorts, throwing $1M+ parties, drinking $1000 bottles of wine, and buying $1M+ pieces of jewelry and art, they should act out their advocacy and give away that which makes their economic circumstances so disparate from their fellow man.

In regard to the liberals' attitude to treat everyone respectfully, as equal brothers in the human race, here again there is a massive contrast in the ideology espoused, and the actions taken in the real world. Most movie stars are extremely arrogant people. They expect to be pampered by everyone they touch including all members of their production crews. Most don't have respect for their families, as they are constantly changing partners and usually have little time for their children. As a group, their private and work lifestyle does not live up to their ideology.

The wealthy corporate raiders or financiers who consider themselves to be liberal, like George Soros, have little social conscience also. They don't care if their financial transactions disrupt economies or sovereign nations. Their jobs also force them to revamp companies, by firing unproductive workers without pre-arranging new jobs for them.

The next group, the wealthy business men also aren't affected by their political bend in their business dealings. Their job forces them to be as competitive, and to make as much profit as possible. Workers' salaries are not equal. And, business protocol requires subservience to the bosses. In addition, when inefficient competitors are put out of business, there is no mourning for the workers put out of work, or the capital loss inflected on the owners. The successful businessman is one whose job is to destroy less competitive businesses. To be competitive, he is willing to step on anyone and everything in the path to success. Steve Jobs is a prime example of the successful businessman. He had no concern about doing whatever it took to make Apple the great success. In the business world, the successful businessman needs to compete with low prices and good service. He needs to fire the incompetent and those lacking in business and social skills, in order to compete. Yet, these same people voice concern over the well-being of the worker in their ideology.

Finally, let's look at the wealthy liberal politicians' treatment of their fellow man. In the elections just run (2018), the liberal politicians labeled the conservatives as women haters, racists, war mongers, and wealthy robber barons. The running of this campaign was in direct contrast with those equalitarian and brotherly love views espoused by their utopian liberal view of mankind. The nation's conservatives represent over 40% of the voting public. So, if the liberals actually believe that man is a benevolent species, and therefore would live according to an idealist's philosophy, how can they be reconciled to the fact that over 40% of the population supports leaders that don't share that viewpoint? Also, how can they reconcile the fact that their own political leaders (who must also be benevolent) didn't have a second thought before unmercilessly attacking conservatives and their agenda.

The lifestyles of the rich and famous liberals are contradictory to their philosophy and their talking points. In reality, they are just hypocritical snake oil salesmen. When they start to act like Mother Teresa, only then should the world listen and respect them. Until then, the economic, social and political policies that these people will try to put in place will lead to disaster. Policies based on the erroneous assumption that self-interest is evil and must be controlled by government, has led to the growth of unified power in government, big business, and big unions. To arrive at fairness to all, the liberals will aspire to use more regulation and taxation to insure their view of society comes to pass. This will lead to more growth in government, along with massive power. And, as we all know, power corrupts. And absolute power corrupts absolutely.

Many liberals are romantics. They are idealistic in their dreams, if not in their personal behavior. Reality isn't what it is, but what it should be. The leaders of this movement however are mainly power grabbers using the liberal illusion to achieve their political aspirations. Although, the liberal (socialistic) concept of creating fairness is totally disruptive and unworkable, these leaders continue to promote a deadly fairy tale. And, unfortunately the main media outlets have fallen under this romantic spell. The liberal propaganda outlet has been unleashed to capture American minds. Our forefathers would be aghast at how Freedom of the Press is being used!!!

ARGUMENT 14
The Perfect Socialistic Setting – The Family

Shouldn't socialism thrive in the family setting, where all family members have the most interest in sharing and each other's happiness? The family is the most basic core of society. Assets held by a married couple are usually equally co-owned and liabilities are also equally shared. The children rely on the parents to provide for them, and most likely will inherit the wealth created by their parents. There is expectation that all members of the family will look out for each other throughout their lives. This sounds like the perfect socialistic setting. One would think testing core socialistic assumptions in the family environment would likely verify their veracity. One would expect that sharing and happiness and no strife would be the dominant behavior if key socialistic assumptions about human attributes were true.

Divorce statistics show that today almost 50% of new marriages result in divorce. Even though sharing would be expected in a married couple, many times married couples deem the allocation of money unfair in respect to each parties' contribution to the family's well-being. Many divorces result from one of the spouses feeling unfairly treated in regard to money issues. And, siblings very rarely share wealth as adults. They consider what they earned on their own or inherited to be their own assets. If there is a large discrepancy in wealth among siblings (regardless of its origin), usually it causes tremendous damage to the relationships involved. Sharing is not natural so even in the family setting, where it should thrive, it doesn't. The socialistic concepts that would be expected to flourish in a family environment don't work.

The self-interest and jealousy traits in humans are so dominate that even in the ideal environment, socialistic concepts don't work. In society, in general, where the individual has very little in common with his fellow man, what will give rise to the concept working better? Allocation of wealth as a fairness concept hasn't worked in any society. The capitalistic concept of allocation by achievement has built the wealthiest society in history where the poor live better than the kings of yesteryear.

Conclusion

The Argument Points above have highlighted the key assumptions and arguments that are made by liberals advocating socialism. The main argument that emanates from the liberal is that a more altruistic social (economic and political) system would be better for mankind. Since most societies promote a Christian like moral philosophy (love thy neighbor, be honest and truthful, selfishness is bad, etc.), the socialistic philosophy would appear to have many positive merits. The arguments against socialism found in the above discussion points evaluates the real nature of man vs. the idealist nature in man. By assuming that the world operates on realism, and not on idealistic assumptions, this chapter provides reasoning why large long-term experiments in socialism have failed, and why capitalism is such a superior economic system.

Unfortunately, the seductiveness of something or everything for free continues to overwhelm many individuals who want to believe in fairy tales. The call for socialism continues to gain strength. What will happen to the economy if the voting electorate is swayed.

CHAPTER 4

The Democrat's 2020 'FREE' Platform - Democratic Socialism at work

A merica could already be considered a socialistic country, in that it provides a good portion of its wealth in attempting to better the lives of the not so well off. In addition, the government mandates hundreds of thousands of rules concerning the environment, hiring practices, safety rules, and business practices, discrimination, etc. These rules act as a form of control over many business decisions by limiting revenue generating avenues, while also increasing the cost structure of business. And, governmental taxation of businesses essentially gives government an ownership position in all U.S. businesses (taxation is profit sharing by the government without ownership).

However, with 25% of GDP spent on social programs, the Democratic party believes that isn't nearly enough. Current leaders of the democratic party are calling for free college education, free total healthcare, universal child care, a much higher minimum wage, and universal basic income as a way to uplift the individuals not making enough. They are also concerned with climate change, and want to change the rules of the energy industry.

Democrats are not only proposing more spending on the lower class, their proposals are aimed at managing more of the economy through a takeover of the health care sector (17% of GDP). And, their proposal (The Green New Deal) for major new rules in the energy and the building industries mean the Democrats want the government in control of these other 2 major industries (6% for energy, 4% for construction). These proposals reflect the Democrats view of how America will become a truly extreme socialistic nation.

America has thrived as basically a capitalistic nation in spite of its 90-year drift towards socialism. The capitalistic incentive to run your own business, and to make exceptional incomes still exists in 2019. Increased government payments to the unfortunate haven't dampened the spirit of the entrepreneurs of our country. However, the current Democratic platform, if implemented, would seriously erode the entrepreneurial incentive. And, it would also undermine the confidence of capitalists doing business in American.

The Democrats are proposing to seriously increase the tax rate (top marginal federal tax going from 37% to 70%) on successful individuals. Their plans of a defacto government takeover of 3 major industries, now put the government in the business of running businesses with a massive increase in regulation.

In regard to the healthcare industry, in a single government payer system (universal healthcare), the insurance industry won't be the prime payer of health care services any longer. And, it likely goes out of business. All doctors' autonomy disappears. And, all health care choices for patients disappear. The government controls everything from doctors' pay to prescription prices, to health facility costs, to treatment options, to scheduling patient services, to wrongful treatment lawsuits, etc. The government becomes the monopoly of health care. And, government officials will run this monopoly of essential societal services with an unfathomable number of rules (government's first attempt to gain partial control of healthcare, Obamacare, needed 20,000 pages of regulations. Total control would mean multiple more rules).

Business monopolies were outlawed in America with the Sherman Act of 1890, the Clayton Act of 1914 and the Federal Trade Commission Act of 1914. Laws against monopolies were instituted to promote competition for the benefit of the consumer. Most Americans would agree that these laws were essential to the well-being of American consumers for the past 100 years. So, how does creating a monopoly for health services by the government promote competition and the best healthcare service for Americans? It does exactly the opposite!!

Democrats argue that universal health care is better than the current system because the government doesn't have the profit motive which has caused healthcare services (or health insurance) to be overpriced. With the cost of healthcare rising much faster than inflation for the past 30 years, the public has grown fed up with the healthcare industry. And, many are biting on the Democrats' argument.

However, their argument is just as fallacious as the argument for egalitarianism, as it is the same argument. The word 'profit', because of 50 years of socialistic training in the American educational system, has a very negative connotation. However, 'profit' and 'incentive' are synonyms for each other in the economic environment. Profit has provided the incentive for hard work, and investment incentive has created the massive increase in human productivity. The Democratic party ignores this fact in choosing to propagandize the bad connotation of 'profit'. As discussed in the previous chapter, incentives drive production and innovation. And, a decrease in incentives will cause production and progress to deteriorate. The Democratic argument that eliminating profit will cause a more productive healthcare system is totally incorrect. In fact, it will lead to a serious decline in the quantity and quality of American healthcare.

Healthcare is just like any other business. Healthcare provides needed services to society. And, business monopolies are bad for the public. Aside from the anti-monopoly laws that were passed acknowledging that monopolies were bad, the government run Post Office (a monopoly before FedEx) is a clear example of inefficiency. The Post Office has never run on a 'profit' motive while FedEx does. Yet, FedEx is the go to supplier of postal services in the world, because of the motivation to run it better for higher profits.

If healthcare services were allowed to run as free enterprise services, the cost of healthcare would drop dramatically and solutions to healthcare problems would be discovered more quickly. However, most of the healthcare industry today isn't subject to serious competition. There is some, but government regulations have massively restricted it. To completely eliminate any competition is a recipe for disaster.

There are five main reasons for the dramatic rise in America's healthcare costs.

The first is the tremendous treatment advancements in healthcare in the last 50 years. In the 1960s (and obviously before), there were no good treatments for heart disease or cancer. Overall life expectancy for all Americans has increased by 4.7 years due to the new treatments for heart disease! The 5-year survival rate of cancer victims has increased by about 30 percentage points in the last 50 years. The treatment programs for both these diseases is expensive and didn't exist in the 1960s. Individuals weren't treated then. And, they died much sooner, alleviating their healthcare costs for the last years of their lives. In addition to these two major advancements, joint replacement surgery also didn't exist in the 1960s. This other major advancement in mankind's quality of living is also expensive. Many other expensive medical advancements have also contributed to the rise in healthcare costs.

The second reason contributing to the increase in healthcare costs is the massive increase in American diabetes. The last 50 years have seen a 7-fold increase in the percentage of Americans with a diabetic condition. Care for diabetes now runs at 7% of the overall cost of healthcare.

The third reason is America's aging population. The median age of Americans is 38.2 years today vs. 29.5 in 1960. Americans over 60 now represent over 20% of the population vs. 13% in 1960. And, healthcare spending by Americans over 60 is over 46% of the total spending on American healthcare. So, people over 60 spend over 2.25 times more than younger people.

The fourth reason for the massive increase in healthcare spending is Americans are wealthy enough to afford the increased cost of taking care of their health. Instead of choosing businesses to pay them higher wages, Americans opted for their employers to pay for health insurance. In 1960, a small percentage of the population had insurance vs. 91% in 2017. Because of the increase in American prosperity, Americans could afford to take better care of themselves through their employer vs. letting life take its course, as was the case for many Americans in 1960.

The last reason for the massive increase in the cost of healthcare is government regulation, which was almost non-existent in 1960. Massive regulation has caused the healthcare industry to become an uncompetitive industry. An article from the MISES INSTITUTE by Mike Holly on 5/9/17 (see appendix) details how government regulation has restricted the supply of medical services, doctors, hospitals, insurance, and pharmaceuticals while subsidizing the demand for these services through governmental payments. The economic discussion of this article details why governmental regulation of supply and demand has been responsible for a large portion of the increase in healthcare costs over the past 50 years, at double the rate of inflation.

The Democrats proposal for universal healthcare, paid for by the government, will increase the demand for American healthcare services, as the consumer will think that these services are free. And, when there is no restriction on demand because it is 'free', the demand will explode (Offering a product for free is the prime method of businesses attracting customers to view that product along with their many other products - it induces demand). And, Democrats are telling the public that this service will be free. If the supply of doctors and other medical services is not radically expanded to meet the increased demand, then demand will be unmet. In this inevitable case, rationing will have to take place and a black market for healthcare services will arise. In all countries with universal health care, rationing is part of the system. And, the black market currently exists. It takes the shape of America where the peoples of the world come to fulfill their critical healthcare needs instead of waiting in line in their own country.

The national cost of American healthcare, in response to a governmental policy of universal healthcare, would significantly rise from the 18% of GDP it currently represents. Since government is paying for these services, it can and will also determine the extent of the increase in spending by creating a governmental budget for healthcare. The budget will determine the total amount allowable to spend each year on healthcare.

Legislators, as stated in a previous paragraph, will detail an encyclopedia of rules and regulations that bureaucratic administrators and regulators will be mandated to follow.

As with all governmental laws, almost no deviation from the prescribed procedure of the law will be allowed, no matter how stupid (the tens of thousands of regulations can't be perfect). Government officials will say 'if you don't like the law, then have it changed - otherwise you have to comply with the law'. And, healthcare patients will be stuck having to adhere to rationing, the bureaucratic method prescribed as the treatment option, the doctor that is assigned to them, and worse - non treatment for critical illnesses (all universal healthcare countries evaluate the cost of treating patients vs. the benefit society will receive from these patients if successfully treated. If the benefit is less than the cost, these countries programs deny treatment).

Americans will lose all the options currently available to them, to take care of themselves. Remember a socialistic society is not concerned with individuality, it is concerned with the conformity that makes everyone equal. So, what is good for the individual isn't as important as what is good for 'society'. The cost of healthcare to society also will be more important than having all individuals' needs served. So, the extent of rationing of services will depend on what the government thinks is the most beneficial spend (% of GDP) for the country. And, the politicians voting for a government run system will have more tax dollars (due to a much bigger government budget) to allocate to the special interest groups that in the long run make all powerful politicians rich (by corrupting them).

The massive rise in the cost of American healthcare in the last 20 years has created a fear in most Americans. They fear that if they lost their employer paid insurance, they would not be able to afford health care for themselves and their families in the future. And, for self-employed individuals and small businesses, the cost of healthcare insurance has become so expensive that it has become unaffordable in many cases. This fear is driving Americans to seek the panacea of an alternative, universal governmental healthcare promised by the Democrats.

The Democrats propaganda machine has blamed the high cost of healthcare on the profits of the insurance industry. And, the propaganda advertised states that a universal coverage plan will eliminate these profits. And, a non-profit provider will make healthcare more affordable. The 8 biggest health insurance providers reported their profits for the 3rd quarter of 2018. They earned a combined $3.3 billion dollars.

In 37 states, the 3 largest insurance providers hold an 80% share of the market. So, it is rational to assume that the 8 biggest insurance providers would hold over 80% of the national market. Using these numbers, a rational assumption could be made that the yearly profits of all health insurance providers would be less than 4 (quarters of profit) times $3.3B times 1.25 (increase 80% to 100%) or $16.5 billion. With the nation spending more than $3.5 trillion dollars on yearly healthcare, $16.5 billion of profits represents less than 2 tenths of 1 percentage of total spending.

Since the profits of the healthcare insurance industry are such a small percentage of total health care spending, it is clear that the American public is being duped into believing that universal health care is the solution to the high cost of health care. In fact, the solution being proposed, by lying politicians, will create much more expensive healthcare, with rationing as part of the process.

Bureaucratic decisions, as a proxy for the rules of delivering healthcare, instead of businesses seeking to improve their profit margins by lowering costs and seeking customer satisfaction will lead to a severe decline in the quality and quantity of healthcare services. Voting for a Democratic plan because of the fear of the high cost of healthcare will boomerang on those seeking to insure themselves of the availability of good healthcare.

Society has been indoctrinated (by the liberal media and liberal educational system) into believing that health care is too vital to human existence to be allowed to be run by evil businessmen. The same argument could be made for the food supply (as it was in Russia and China). The capitalistic system made Thomas Malthus (the leading economic scholar of the 1800s) and his predictions of the impending catastrophic future world food shortage crisis look ridiculous (although the world population has gone up 7 fold in the last 200 years, there is an abundance of food today). The extreme socialists in Russia and China expropriated farming from the farmers because food production was a vital industry. But instead of increasing the food supply, the expropriation caused massive famines in both countries. So, if government control of this vital industry didn't pan out as a good idea, why would government control of the healthcare industry result in being a good decision by a society that votes for it?

Socialized medicine or universal healthcare is one of the legs of the Democrat platform to convince Americans that more governmental control will create a better system. When analyzed in depth, this policy leg fails the cost and productivity test (economics 101). It will act as the opposite of a panacea for a less costly better healthcare system. What about the other leg of the Democratic platform, the Green New Deal, that aims at the takeover of the energy and construction industries?

The Green New Deal, like the proposal for universal healthcare, is another attempt by politicians to control more of the economy (The government budget increases with more governmental control. And politicians in partnerships with special interests gain more influence in the economy. This increased influence is translated into more big bucks for the bank accounts of the rule makers).

The Green New Deal is premised on the human race becoming extinct in a few short years if current carbon dioxide emissions aren't controlled. Global warming is based on the premise that increasing carbon dioxide levels in the atmosphere increasingly traps more energy in the earth's ecosystem by not allowing it to be released into space.

After calculating the amount of carbon dioxide in the atmosphere each year, and also calculating the earth's average temperature in recent history, many scientists arrived at a calculation that expresses their theory of the current warming trend on earth. Globally, the researchers saw an average temperature increase of $1.7 \pm 0.4°C$ per trillion tonnes of carbon in CO_2 emissions (TtC), which was supposedly consistent with reports from the Intergovernmental Panel on Climate Change. According to researchers, there was approximately 600 million tonnes of carbon emissions in the atmosphere at the end of 2015.

So, based on current emissions, temperature, according to these researchers, is expected to rise by .067 of 1 degree every year in the future. After 3 years of added emissions since this published study, this number should be around 700 million tonnes today. These added emissions would increase the rate of temperature increase by .16 and make it .083 of 1 degree per year. And, with the current rate of emissions - 37.1M tons - this will theoretically increase warming by an additional .0041 degree every year.

The Green New Deal proclaims that the world has 12 years to take drastic action to avoid the 'existential threat' (temperatures too high to maintain man's level of existence on the earth) of climate change. And, since it is assumed that businesses run for profit won't do anything to prevent this forthcoming disaster, then the government must exercise its muscle to save the world. Democrats propose that by taking over the energy industry, they will cut the use of fossil fuels, and replace these fuels with green energy (solar, wind, geothermal, etc.). Thus, the impending crisis will be solved. And, Democrats imply, in their narrative, that the American public's standard of living will not be effected.

There are three major problems to this Democratic solution to save the world, even if the demise of earth because of global climate change was a reality. The first problem is that the U.S. emits only 15% (5.4 gigatons of US emissions vs. 37.1 gigatons for the world) of total world emissions. So, any unilateral action by the U.S. will have little effect on the time line that is proclaimed to be catastrophic. If the U.S. cut emissions by 50%, or 2.7 gigatons, it wouldn't even add 1 year to the experts' forecasted 12 years before warming would increase world temperature by 1 degree (A 50% cut would put U.S. per capita emissions in line with Europe's emissions).

There is no reasonable amount of short term energy cutting, and additions of green energy, that America can do to seriously change the catastrophic outcome that the 'experts' predict. Politicians claim that if the U.S. sets the example of seriously (which is undefined by them) acting on climate change, then the rest of the world will follow (to what extent is undefined).

The Paris Accord supposedly was the agreement document that would move the world to salvation. Three years since the Agreement was signed in October 2016, none of the major developed nations, which account for about 25% of global emissions, have met their pledged emission reductions. And, those initial pledged cuts, if made, would have been much too little to meet the goal of keeping global warming under 2 degrees by the year 2100 (the goal of the Paris Accord). Studies showed that even with the pledged cuts, temperature would increase by 3 degrees instead. The fact is that the citizens of the world don't want to sacrifice their current standard of living by diverting investment dollars to a 'theoretical' cause. Instead, the peoples of the world want investment to increase their quality of life.

The western world has a much higher standard of living than China, India, and the rest of the world. Yet, because of the huge population in the rest of the world, Europe and the U.S. only emit approximately 25% of carbon emissions. So, even if the citizens of the western world accepted a lower standard of living to fight climate change, the rest of the world would also need to be convinced to accept their plight in living conditions to help save the world. The Paris Accord understood that asking the poor to stay poor would never fly. So, the Agreement asks the developed countries not only to pay for cutting emissions in their own countries, but also in the underdeveloped countries.

The lack of investment made, since the signing, for climate change by the countries of the Paris Accord show that both developing and underdeveloped countries are more concerned with increasing their standard of living today than worrying about climate change effecting their future welfare. As energy is a prime component in increasing economic output, it can only be assumed that world energy consumption will rise with the world's attempt for more economic progress, especially in the underdeveloped countries. If Europe's emissions per capita is considered a benchmark for CO_2 emissions (7 tonnes per person), a world per capita rate of that much would mean today's world emissions would increase by 38% or an additional 14.2B tons emitted per year. And, temperatures would increase by 1 degree every 11 years instead of every 12. Even if the rest of the world only increased emissions by 15% in the next 12 years, this would just offset the U.S. cut (This calculation is an under-estimation since world population is expected to grow by 900M people or 12% in the next 10 years).

The second problem in the Democrat's Green Deal is that the cost of green energy is at least 25% more (wikipidea) than the cost of fossil fuels, although these calculations do not include externalities such as health damage by coal plants, nor the effect of CO_2 emissions on the climate, ocean acidification, and eutrophication, and ocean current shifts. Not only do studies verify that green energy is more expensive than fossil fuels, the governments of the world have had to incentivize the use of green energy through subsidies of around 30%.

Because individuals' current standards of living are almost considered a right in America (especially by Democrats) and in western Europe, convincing Americans (or Europeans) to reduce their living conditions to benefit the future is an almost impossible task. By switching energy sources to more costly energy sources, the citizens of the developed world must necessarily become victims to a lower standard of living. And, in the last 3 years, since the Paris Accord was signed, the lack of government spending on climate change indicates that their citizens have no stomach for sacrifice. In fact, in France, huge protests arose when the government tried to impose a tax on fuel to just reduce this source of emissions.

The third problem is that not only is alternative green energy much more expensive than fossil fuels such as natural gas, but changing the infrastructure of energy production will be very costly. And, it would take many decades to accomplish. In 2018, the U.S. generated over 1.2 million megawatts of power of which 14% was green energy. About 4100 of these plants, each generating 250MW of power, would need to be built to replace the U.S. current generation system to become a zero emissions nation. Based on the cost of building current plants, the cost to build out plant and equipment for 1 million megawatts would be 100,000,000 times $2644 per kilowatt or 2.644 trillion dollars.

And, another 2100 for the rest of power used (ex. - electric cars to replace gasoline) in the U.S. would cost .49 times $2.64 trillion or another 1.29T dollars.

Currently, studies show that to build a new utility scale solar power plant (250MV) would take six years. The resources needed to build 6200 such plants, in regard to planners, available sites, environmental issues, constructions workers, building materials, financing issues and regulatory body approvals would be too overwhelming to make America a zero emissions country in a short period of time. Leading Democrats have said that Americans have 12 years to make the change to zero emissions, or catastrophe will strike. This is the reason they give to justify having the government take over the energy industry.

However, a zero emissions U.S. doesn't come close to solving the world's 'theoretical' catastrophic problem of global warming. So, the Democrat's claim, that taking over the energy industry will provide a solution to climate change, is a huge lie. Politicians want more power through a bigger government that they control. If the energy industry is run by government, it will be a monopoly run for the interests of the politicians and their lobbyist, not for the benefit of America in general.

If the 'global warming scientists' are right in their predictions, the world is facing a massive problem. Currently, even with the enormous information push of this narrative throughout the world, not enough people believe in the predictions to seriously change their economic behavior.

Although almost all politicians are promoting green energy, they are not insisting on a carbon tax to make green energy truly competitive. They know the public isn't ready to sacrifice. And these politicians don't want to lose their jobs. Instead of being honest with the public, the Democratic narrative is that the energy industry is making so much money, that eliminating the industry through government takeover will allow for green energy to become affordable. Energy industry profits will no longer be part of the energy cost (this is the same false argument as that being made concerning universal healthcare).

Politicians are expert con artists. So, it is no surprise that they are lying about the economic cost of fixing the problem of 'global warming'. If the science is accurate, the economic consequences for the world will be severe. Either the current response will be inadequate, or a full blown response will cause massive economic disruption. The only way to mitigate the consequences would be the development of new energy technology that is cost effective and easily implemented. A U.S. government takeover of the energy industry would be counter-productive to realizing this objective. Dramatically increasing the private sector's incentive to find a solution would be much more productive. Innovation and invention have always been best served by entrepreneurs.

The second leg, the takeover of energy industry, of the Democratic platform doesn't pass the common sense test. The first leg, universal healthcare didn't pass either. The other less substantial parts of the Democratic platform, student loan forgiveness, free college education, universal child care, and universal basic income also don't make any common sense. 'The Garden of Eden', where everything was free, ended soon after it began. And since, man has had to work hard to survive. When everything is free, there is no incentive to work or to invest in new methodology to increase production. If elected, Democrats implementing what they preach will drastically reduce incentives. And, it will therefore reduce production. And that will lead to a depression.

The free programs highlighting the Democrats 2020 policy agenda are aimed at reducing the enormous wealth gap found in America today. Giveaways such as food stamps, housing for the poor, etc., haven't worked in the past to reduce America's wealth gap. Not only wouldn't the current proposal work, implementation of the Democratic agenda will lead to the collapse of the economy.

It doesn't take the mind of a rocket scientist to look at the facts and come to the conclusion that true socialism is a horrible idea. It will always lead to economic decay. The current radical economic agenda being proposed by the Democratic party is very socialistic.

This agenda, however, may moderate before the 2020 elections, if the more rational part of the party obtains power. So, instead of the demand for government to essentially take control of the energy and health sectors, the more moderate agenda might just be to reverse Trump's tax cuts, amend Obamacare, and put on a carbon tax. The more moderate Democrats will be still seeking to control the healthcare and energy industry through taxes, rules and regulation. They will also be seeking to reduce wealth discrepancy in America through similar measures. Can the continued moderated march toward socialism that started in the 1930s make any sense?

CHAPTER 5

Arranging the chairs on the Titanic

Today, government controls 35% to 40% of the economy. And, with all the regulations that were imposed prior to the presidency of Trump, government likely had a say in another 20% to 30% of the economy. This amount of governmental control led to the financial crisis of 2008. A depression was averted by government bailing out the banks and the financial system, by lowering interest rates from a 50-year average of about 5% to close to zero percent, and by initiating new government spending programs of close to $1T per year. Even with this massive government support, the economic recovery was the worst recovery of the last 70 years.

President Trump cut regulations by eliminating thousands of laws. And, President Trump's policy of turning around the elitists' policy of 'Globalism' to 'America First' was instrumental in bringing back hundreds of thousands of manufacturing jobs to America. Government's strangle hold on business, especially small business, was loosened. And, this has led to an extremely strong economic recovery, which is reflected in the lowest unemployment rate in the U.S. since 1960.

The economy is booming but there are still major problems on the horizon. The economy is being pumped up by yearly deficit spending of 5% of GDP. And, federal government debt is over $23T, which is over 100% of GDP. These economic factors could be overcome with good government policy. However, $45T is estimated to be the present value of future unfunded debt. Adding this liability to the current federal debt brings overall government debt to $68T or a whopping 350% of GDP. With American obligations at this extreme level, there is no room for any governmental policy error.

The Democratic agenda of taxing the rich, and giving away most of everything for free is a huge economic policy error. The economic consequences will be of a magnitude that will surpass that of America's Great Depression. Instead of being concerned with deadly icebergs, the Democrats policy is arranging for the rich and poor to sit together on the Titanic.

CHAPTER 6

The problem with Guilty feelings

A t the conclusion of Chapter 1, the following question was asked - So, should the discussion point being addressed be the one about the 'fairness' of a huge divide in wealth between the rich and the poor or should it be, what economic system is most beneficial to the poor as well as society in general? The logical answer is that an economic system that benefits all of society is better than one which strives for equal benefits for everyone, but produces substantially less for all.

However, this logical answer doesn't address the sympathetic cord in many people who feel guilty for having substantially more than those seeking handouts on the street. Homelessness in America is an unacceptable condition to Americans. Also, poverty that causes people to live in squalor and starvation isn't acceptable. As America is the richest country in the world, there doesn't seem to be a reason for these conditions to exist. When Americans see the huge wealth divide in the country, their rational, abetted by Democratic rhetoric, is to blame the rich. And, in believing that dialog, they move toward more governmental control and socialism.

Somehow, 90 years after the Great Depression and with much greater empathy from the country for public assistance, vast increases in government spending haven't been a solution for eliminating the poor. The reason for this is that the core principles of America are independence and freedom. The current assistance programs, run by the government, are therefore restricted from requiring the participants to give up any of their American rights. The homeless are allowed to live wherever they wish. And, they are allowed to carry on their lives as they see fit, as long as no serious law violations are committed. As tolerance for the homeless behavior has grown, most minor offenses (such as using the streets as the toilet, minor shoplifting, etc.) are not prosecuted. The homeless and poor are portrayed as victims of society. And, according to the PC (politically correct) culture, victims require sympathy and a right to the public trough.

Independence requires the individual to fend for himself without reliance on others. Yet, government programs foster dependency while still trying to adhere to a policy allowing individual independence. The objectives of such policies are counter to each other. So, the policy makes no sense. That is why these policies have failed to be productive.

Unfortunately, the top governmental policy makers' main objective isn't to spend the tax payers' dollars efficiently for the overall good of the nation. Their objective is to satisfy special interests groups (who make money from government contracts, etc.) in order to get reciprocal treatment. It's not easy to flaunt the voters' common sense when an issue is simple. So, policy makers turn simple issues into very complex issues by adding numerous variables. Law makers tie many unrelated subjects together in one bill so that common sense is constrained. The problem of homelessness has a simple solution. However, the solutions provided by our lawmakers are counter-productive. The solutions have been to give out more benefits, which leads to more dependence. Instead, the homeless need to learn to be independent. And, they should be forced into training programs that will guarantee jobs and independence on successful completion.

There are three reasons causing the majority of the homeless problem. Mental health problems, drug abuse, and job loss are the main causes of the problem. Without special programs, these individuals will most likely remain homeless and dependent on some sort of public support currently in place (free meals, temporary housing, etc.). By not forcing these men and women off the streets, they will remain there. Should they have the right to this freedom?

Liberals and progressives argue that the Constitution grants every American the right to live life as he chooses. However, the Constitution doesn't suggest that society (government) has to support anyone's lifestyle. In fact, the government left all charity work to private institutions prior to the 1900s. Since the 1930s, government has gotten into the business of taking care of its citizens. It has also become intrusive into regulating the behavior of its citizens with hundreds of laws. So, the liberal argument, that it is unconstitutional to remove the homeless from the streets, is not consistent with other implemented governmental policy.

Minors are taken away from their families if child services deem the parents unfit. And, these minors are put in foster homes since they are deemed to be incapable of taking care of themselves. It is clear that the homeless have lost the ability to take care of themselves. So, why shouldn't they also be put in someone else's care? When minors turn 18, they become adults. And, they no longer are subject to the rules of their foster home. Homeless adults, when they land a job that will support them, should also return to independence.

It is evident that homeless adults will need help in finding a job. Most likely, they don't have the skills required by the current fast changing economy. They may have a drug problem that prevents their employment. And, they also may not want to move to a different part of the country where their skills are still in demand. None of today's governmental policies force the homeless into finding a job, or force them into programs that will lead to that result.

Solving the homeless problem is helping them get a job by forcing them to take relevant training education, forcing them to become sober, and forcing them to move to viable job markets. The mentally ill should be helped by removing them from the street, and putting them in an appropriate facility for treatment.

Since these programs don't currently exist, programs to train and then place graduates with jobs needs to be created. The cost of these programs should be equally shared by the states in accordance with their populations. And, the facilities to house, feed, and train should be located in low cost areas of the country, in order keep costs down. Once a graduate is placed with a job, he no longer would have any obligation to the government.

The current public assistance programs aren't working. These programs only produce long-term dependency. And, as technology is rapidly changing the workplace environment, the need to retrain the workforce increases dramatically. Without programs specifically aimed at doing this, the homeless problem will only grow larger. And, dependency and poverty are closely related. Poverty will only end when everyone works.

The idea of independence and freedom rests on the belief that people can take care of themselves. This idea has been a core principle of the United States. However, America has been moving away from this idea since the presidency of Franklin Roosevelt. Since 2008, the idea of dependence (socialism) has become the mainstream idea to replace independence. America's educational system, in the last 30 years, has been overtaken by socialistic educators. The result of these factors is that in spite of overwhelming evidence that only capitalism leads to a much improved standard of living, Americans are still indoctrinated to view socialism as attractive.

Also, the fact that government has expanded enormously in the past 90 years is mistakenly correlated to the massive increase in Americans' standard of living. Government doesn't produce products. Only, businesses do. Unfortunately, many voters are constantly told that government policy is responsible for the economic outcome of the economy. So, they think that government is responsible for the actual production in the economy. It is true that taxation and regulation policies have an enormous effect on business production. Less regulation and taxation lead to business expansion while the opposite leads to business contraction. The more incentives a business has to produce, the more it will produce. More governmental control of business through socialistic policies reduces business' incentives to produce.

Empathy for the poor, hate or distaste for the rich, a socialistic narrative (education and the mainstream media) from birth to grave, and the false perception that government is in the production business have led many Americans to forget that capitalism is solely responsible for their current high standard of living. Government has been unable to solve the poverty problem in America. So, the private sector should be delegated this task. Incentives should be given to industry to tackle the problem.

President Trump's program of 'Opportunity Zones', where capital gain tax breaks are given to investors in depressed parts of the country, is the first government backed program to have business help in solving the poverty problem.

Enormous wealth gaps between the rich and the poor have historically always existed in every type of society. However, no other economic systems have ever resulted in the major elevation of all its citizens' standard of living. Wealth disparity that is obtained by satisfying human needs is a far superior system than a system that leads to equal sharing, but of a shortage of goods. There are poverty problems in America. But it isn't the capitalistic system that produces them. 90 years of empathetic socialistic governmental policy hasn't eliminated poverty. Creating more giveaway programs by aggressively becoming more socialistic will destroy capitalistic incentives and result in less for all (including the poor). Instead, the capitalistic system should be embraced and provided incentives to eliminate unemployment and poverty.

Empathy and sympathy for the poor and homeless is part of humanity. Handouts to these people, as a solution to relieve their immediate condition, is the simple solution injected into the American system to resolve Americans' guilty. Handouts without conditions is socialistic policy that doesn't work. Setting conditions is part of capitalism. The Bible says don't give fish to the poor, teach them how to fish. In order for the continued improvement in the life of the poor, they must be taught how to care for themselves. So, human kindness dictates a capitalistic approach to improving the lives of everyone.

CHAPTER 7

Human kindness vs. the evil white men socialistic narrative

L eading socialists, as well as any educated person, must know that capitalism is a far better system of delivering economic success to society. However, for politicians, it is easier to maintain power and control of the population in a socialistic government. And, in order to change a democracy (or republic) into a socialistic government, politicians must convince the voter that capitalism is only good for a small percentage of people, the rich.

Socialists focus on the wealth gap in capitalistic countries (even though it has existed throughout history no matter which economic or political system was in place) to prove that the average citizen is not getting his fair share. In addition, socialists tell their audience what a fair share is. A fair share today is touted as all citizens are entitled to healthcare from birth to grave. They are entitled to decent housing and food. They are entitled to a free education through college. They are entitled to child care. And, the list goes on and on. Most everything that the rich enjoy should be enjoyed by everyone.

If everyone had access to the same standard of living as the rich, then the incentive to be rich would disappear (Why would anyone work if there wasn't a significant reward for doing so?). As discussed earlier, this would lead to a massive drag on the economic system. And, the abundance produced by the capitalistic system would disappear. This rational truth, verified by history and actual practice, is being totally ignored by the 45% of the America public who favor socialism. The left has done an incredible job of brainwashing them.

Educators, mainstream media, and most of social media have been responsible for this indoctrination. These entities support the narratives of entitlements for everyone, and soak the rich. They also mete out social justice though public ridicule of critics of the left's narrative. Conservatives are subject to extreme personal attacks on their character. The false allegations and accusations are so potent that jobs may be lost and social ostracism is likely to take place. The repercussion of presenting ideas contrary to those held by the left is so severe that rational debate is almost non-existent today. When ideas (or propaganda) go uncontested, they become accepted as being true. In the case of socialism, there was almost no support for it in the 1960s. Today, about 45% of the public supports it.

Helping the left in its push for economic equivalency are other social policies, that are aimed at keeping rational debate at a minimum. The "WOKE" movement plays an instrumental role in the left's agenda to control American thought. Socialism and the WOKE movement are closely tied together. Raven Cras of Blavity News wrote that "The phenomenon of being woke is a cultural push to challenge problematic norms, systemic injustices and the overall status quo through complete awareness. Being woke refers to a person being aware of the theoretical ins and outs of the world they inhabit. Becoming woke, or staying woke, is the acknowledgment that everything we've been taught is a lie_(kind of/mostly)". By challenging the foundations of every aspect of society, including economics, social turmoil is created. And, revolution becomes easier to forment.

The basic premise of the WOKE movement is that all human beings are equal and should be treated as equals in every living, working, and social setting. As equals, humans should also have equal access to all goods and services. Wealth discrepancy is wrong by definition. And, any instance of deferential treatment is wrong. Since one of the main tenants of the Constitution is equality, and equal treatment under the law, the left constantly issues lawsuits to challenge conservative personal behavior, in both public and private settings. There has been a profound change in America's business community, as well as in private communities, because of the constant barrage of lawsuits filed by the left, along with mainstream media pushing for social correctness.

Social activism is taking place in every corner of American society. The explosion of social media has allowed a small percentage of the population to exert tremendous influence in changing American norms and values. The political correctness pushed by social activists and the mainstream media has made gay marriage legal, has made climate change appear catastrophic, has expanded the toxicity and definition of racist behavior, has changed the definition of sexual misconduct, has made national sovereignty appear racist, has provided an excuse for criminality, and has tainted the role of capitalism in drastically raising the world's standard of living. And, most recently, it has blamed the problems of the world on the white man, especially the 'privileged' white American male.

The whole American educational system has been infiltrated by left leaning educators in the last 5 decades. The mainstream media has followed suit, as left leaning university liberal arts courses have produced the writers and commentators of today's news outlets. The recent explosion of politically correct bloggers on social media is providing a final blow to influencing thoughts about the American economic and social system. Conservatism is being squeezed out as a competing narrative for the best system to run a society.

If the social views pushed by the left had significant merit, then the left would be doing a service to America. There is some merit in the arguments for fairer treatment of some Americans. And, everyone would like the human race to be much nicer than history has shown (continual war, torture, prejudice and persecution, murder, rape, lies, etc.).

The truth is that all individuals are mostly self-interested. All the wrongdoings of the world cannot be attributed to just rich capitalists (capitalists in power is just a recent 200 year phenomena), or just the rich in general. The interactions of all mankind's self-interest have been responsible for all that is good and evil in the world. When success (either political, economic, or inherited) leads to overwhelming power, then self-interest likely corrupts those in power. A widely accepted axiom is power corrupts and absolute power corrupts absolutely. The socialistic narrative is that capitalistic power has corrupted society. And, socialism implicitly states that government should be the most powerful entity in society, instead of business, so as to prevent this corruption.

However, in the history of the world, corrupt capitalism (whenever it existed) controlled much less power than kingdoms, aristocracies, emperors, communism, or the Roman Republic. A corrupt government should be feared much more than a corrupt capitalistic society.

The rich didn't turn a good percentage of the population into savages. The rulers of the world today aren't solely white rulers. White supremacy didn't exist throughout much of history. And, white privilege wasn't enjoyed by the serfs of the European royalty. Mankind's self-interest, savage and intolerant behavior didn't arise because of the ruling rich. It is the natural behavior of all species, 'survival of the fittest', as theorized by Darwin.

The left's false underlying premise, that only the rich (now the white rich) have ruined the world, makes their argument for socialism ridiculous. And, the left's conclusion that the world will be a better place when everyone equally shares in economic output is ridiculous. It ignores that this outcome is based on the false assumption that sharing is natural human behavior. Therefore wealth sharing will reduce the incentive for risk taking and it will reduce people's willingness to work. Without economic incentives, the world's standard of living would never be where it is today.

The incentive for most to be better than past generations, to be better at providing for your family, to be better at work, and to be better at providing solutions to health issues, production issues, and social issues is only found in a free capitalistic society. The incentive of economic success far out-weighs sharing and community service as a driver for the betterment of mankind. The philosophy of goodwill to all men (sharing) was originated with Christianity. And, although this religion and other similar religions have been practiced for a couple of thousands years, man's living conditions hardly improved because of it.

How do rational minds believe that healthcare, a good job, a good education, and a high standard of living are part of their rights? How do rational minds believe that everyone should share equally in the consumption of goods regardless of their contribution to producing those goods?

50 years ago, there was no effective treatment for heart disease. If you inherited a heart problem, you died early. The same was true for cancer. And, there were no body part replacement (knees, hips, arteries, kidneys, etc.) therapies. So, if these healthcare procedures weren't available 50 years ago, how could they be a human right?

The massive monetary incentive to solve health issues led to massive investment in healthcare. Without capitalism, healthcare would still be in the dark ages. And, without the incentive (not provided in a socialistic system) to grow and maintain the current healthcare services, the quality of currently practiced medicine will certainly regress. The same is true for all the other 'rights' promoted by socialistic doctrine. Capitalistic incentives have been solely responsible for the incredible standard of living that exists today.

Socialists blame capitalism for all the problems of society. Their arguments ignore the fact that these social problems have existed for all human history, when capitalism didn't exist. Yet, the only system that has dramatically increased mankind's standard of living is capitalism. How can 45% of educated Americans be fooled by the lies of the politicians, educators and the media pushing for more government, and therefore extreme socialism?

Capitalism (labeled greed by the left) unleashed man's creative spirit, imagination, and working energy. The shackles of the class system, where only elitist ideas survived, while contradicting ideas were either left to die or severely criticized, were finally broken by capitalism.

It is sad that appreciation for social and economic freedom has deteriorated to be held by only 55% of the population. And, it is extremely worrisome that the brainwashing of Americans has been so effective. Americans have been educated to read and write. But this education doesn't appear to have given them the ability to think rationally.

Humanity is full of evil people, but getting rich by tremendously improving everyone's standard of living with new great products doesn't constitute wrong doing! When the scam of socialism infiltrates the minds of so many literate voters, it easy to see how mankind's ability to be free is so fleeting. Wake up America!

CHAPTER 8

A capitalistic solution to the ailing American psyche

I t is clear that a major problem exists in America when 45% of the public doesn't like capitalism, and would prefer more socialism. What is bothering many Americans is the uncertainty of the future. Capitalism doesn't promise security but socialism falsely does.

The golden era of American capitalism is perceived to be the years after WWII until the late 1960s. The U.S. economy initially expanded because of pent-up demand following the war. The optimism after the war caused Americans to spend. And, optimism fed on optimism as the economy expanded throughout this period. Job security wasn't an issue as the expanding economy created job opportunities throughout America. Most white collar and blue collar jobs provided a retirement benefit. And, workers weren't worried about their social security benefits. Most workers felt that they could retire somewhat comfortably.

In the late 1960s, competition with Japan caused American factories to close. Because many manufacturing companies faced bankruptcy, the pension payments to many blue collar workers were thrown in jeopardy. And, for the WWII generation, this was the first crack to cause some of those workers to doubt American capitalism. As Japan's economic power receded after 1980, Americans started to feel better about their future. With America's technology revolution expanding rapidly in the

1990s, the future (capitalism) looked bright to most Americans. Unfortunately, the reconstitution of communism created the business opportunity of finding extremely cheaper labor in the Soviet Union and China in the late 1990s. This cheaper labor provided the incentive for American companies to lay off American workers and outsource those jobs. America's elitist class (C-class executives and prominent politicians) jumped all over their shot to greatly increase business profits by substituting foreign labor for domestic labor.

Globalization became the avenue for businesses to follow in the 2000s. 40,000 U.S. factories were shut down. And, 5 million U.S. jobs were lost to foreign countries because of this business policy. Although multi-national corporate business profits soared, domestic businesses suffered from the competition of cheap goods produced overseas. U.S. wages were either capped or declined because of the foreign competition. U.S. unemployment soared to over 13M. And, there was no end in sight until President Trump took office in 2016. It's no wonder that the American public was worried about their job and retirement security. And, socialism (as an alternative to a capitalistic system that wasn't working for the American worker) started to be embraced by more people than just governmental workers (who benefit from a bigger government), and indoctrinated educators.

Big business was cashing in on the labor of the working class. Except, that labor was foreign labor!!! Only big business was benefiting from capitalism. The U.S. workers were not! The model of capitalism benefiting everyone seemed to be breaking down. So, support for it naturally declined. The Democrats used the economic turmoil, caused by globalization, to convince the public that more government was needed. And, this led to the election of Barrack Obama, who promised and delivered more governmental programs to aid average Americans.

With increased federal government spending of around $800B/year, and a lowering of the 50-year average interest rate of about 5% to close to 0%, the economy got better. However, the underlying economic problem of globalism wasn't even questioned by President Obama, the Democrats, or the Republicans. In fact, it was seen as benefiting the American public by reducing the cost of products in America!

The band-aid of massive governmental economic support covered up the economic wound of globalism. However, the support programs caused the federal deficit to increase by around $1T/year. And, if interest rates returned to the average rate in normal times (5%), the annual deficit would go up by an additional $800B/year. The public is happy that times are better. But, they are well aware that huge government deficits could likely lead to major economic problems in the future. This perception has kept the majority of Americans worried about their future financial security. And, because American capitalism has been heavily advertised as the reason for the Great Recession, instead of globalism, socialism has gained the acceptance of 45% of the American population.

Although an analysis of history and logic debunk the myth of socialism as being good economic policy, that hasn't been enough to convince a large percentage of Americans that a much bigger government won't be good for them. And, for some reason, many extremely educated people, professors and teachers, journalists and news commentators, and extremely successful business people like Bill Gates, Michael Bloomberg, and others believe that higher taxes, and more governmental involvement in basic human needs would be better for America.

In a recent interview, Bill Gates made the argument that Americans advocating for more governmental services weren't socialists since government wouldn't own all means of production (the old definition of socialism). He said that these Americans still want capitalism but with a "strong social safety net". He also said, "The majority of rich countries in Europe already have what AOC proposes. That doesn't make them socialists. In any case, it makes them social democrats." "For the younger generations, socialism only means making sure that everyone can go to the doctor when they need it, or have a roof over their heads, or have money to buy food, regardless of that person's circumstances."

When Bill Gates, who must be considered extremely intelligent, says that the demands of AOC (Representative Alexandria Ocasio-Cortez) aren't socialistic, then it is understandable that 45% of Americans who believe in socialism (with a new definition) are on the same page. And, herein lies the problem that America is facing. The 45% of Americans, and many well educated and elite Americans like Mr. Gates, think that providing just a little more for every American won't significantly change the economic dynamics of the country. And, they believe the added benefits will provide the economic security that everyone deserves.

America currently provides services of shelter, food, and healthcare to all Americans. However, the quality of these services is not commensurate with that envisioned by Mr. Gates and other liberals. In general, young middle class liberals want to be assured that the standard of living they have become accustomed to will exist throughout their lives. And, they want that same standard of living for those less privileged than themselves. Poorer young liberals want the same. Older liberals and wealthy liberals also think the current middle class standard of living should be available to everyone. Most liberals therefore believe that the minimal standard of living should be close to the current middle class level. And, they believe that this standard of living should continue throughout life.

So, the first question that needs to be addressed is whether America can afford to provide all its people with a standard of living commensurate with that of the middle class today. Median household income in America was around $63K/year in 2018. A general analysis of data compiled on U.S. household income distribution show that raising the median for those below the median to the median would require around $1.9T/year. Those households above the median have after tax income in excess of about $7T above the median. So, it appears that America is wealthy enough to raise everyone to a lower middle class income level. This might be enough to satisfy liberals.

However, personal savings in America was $1.037T in 2018. So, in order to transfer $1.9T in income from the upper middle class and the rich through taxation policy, those affected would not only have to curtail investment, but also would have to cut their consumption of goods and services. There are 2.5M households that make over $390K/year, or an approximate total income of $985B. And, there are 1.3M households that make over $475K/year, or an approximate total income of $570B. So, even raising taxes by 50 percentage points (to a marginal rate of around 80%) on the wealthiest Americans would only take care of 40% of the required money to raise all American households to a $63K yearly income. Households making around $250K/year (6.9M households) would also require significant tax increases. Each of the 10.7M wealthy households would have to relinquish $177K/year, if the transfer of wealth was equally prorated.

Consumer consumption would increase with a transfer of wealth to the poorer levels of society. And, correspondingly investment would decline. In this case, likely the rich would cut as little as possible from consumption but would make very deep cuts in their investments, since the funds currently available would be stripped from them. As America's investment capability diminished to close to zero, and the incentive to work harder for higher incomes deteriorated, America's economy would fall behind global competition. This would lead to an economic death spiral. And, in not too many years, the majority of American households would earn less than the median income today.

When liberals and Mr. Gates articulate that 'giving just a little more' is not socialism. And, it will alleviate the 'unfairness' of being 'poor', they need to define the living standard that they expect giving 'just a little more' will achieve. America can't afford to raise the income levels of the poor to the lower level of the middle class. A lower household income of less than lower middle class income would still likely lead liberals and Mr. Gates to still think that giving 'just a little more' was justified.

As mentioned in the last chapter, giveaways only help the poor for very short periods of time. And, when freebies and charity becomes constraining on the smartest and hardest working people of society, production of goods and services declines drastically as a result. Giving 'just a little more' results in everyone having a lot less in the long run. Reducing incentives will create lasting pain.

Forcing the dependent poor to get educated, and placing them in a job after achievement of educational success (as discussed in Chapter 5) is the correct governmental policy. Increasing everyone's incentives to be more productive in society will yield enormous benefits. The poor in America today live better than the American middle class of the early 1900s, as proof that incentives work. And, a more productive society will dissipate Americans' concern about their future and help heal their psyche.

CHAPTER 9

Can America reunite?

The American psyche has become extremely fractured in the last 60 years since the Vietnam war. The social positions then were pacifism vs. the establishment's militarism (the industrial/military complex). After the war, pacifism evolved into socialism. And, the industrial/military complex evolved into capitalism. A small percentage of young pacifists became journalists and educators. And, a very small percentage of young people became leaders in industry. The majority of the young followed in their parent's footsteps to become average citizens. However, their youthful experience would make them generally more liberal than their parents.

The tendency for society to become more liberal was accelerated by the influence of leftist leaning journalists and educators, who have dominated those industries. America's 400 years of culture of individualism and independence was virtually unchallenged until the 1960s. Almost all Americans cherished this philosophy. So, the philosophy of socialism (dependence) had a hard time gaining a foothold. Journalists and educators always pushed for more social reform (dependency on the government) but never for outright socialism. Society in the years before 2000 would never have tolerated such advocacy. However, the constant barrage of leftist ideas over a 50 plus year period produced a major crack in Americans' belief in independence. And, this has led to the fracture that exists today in America.

The advocacy of socialism has gained enough support to become a mainstream contender to capitalism, which still retains its support from a slight majority of the population. The philosophy of socialism and capitalism have no common ground. There is no middle road in ideology! And, the clash for dominance has become commonplace. The left's 'take no prisoners strategy' (any criticism of the left's positions on gender rights, no borders policy, abortion, human rights, capitalism, etc.) is met with the severe repercussions of possible job loss, physical harm, social ostracism, boycotting, etc. These repercussions have shut down debate and inflamed an already contentious disagreement between the individuals deciding how society should function.

There can be no doubt that capitalism is the most productive economic system ever devised. It is also the only system that allows complete freedom and independence in the political arena. However, capitalism doesn't carry the guarantee of personal or economic security for all of society. In the dark ages, after the fall of the Roman empire, people chose security over independence to become serfs. This choice created the European monarchies that bled their constituency for over 1,000 years. Socialism promises security, and (falsely) claims there is no cost. And, similar to the dark ages, this argument still sways a lot of people today.

Therefore, even if the socialistic argument is irrational, capitalists and society in general have to pay attention to the thoughts of a significant minority. Revolutions do happen! For this reason, capitalists have capitulated to the demands of the public, as they have allowed increased government spending for the poor to become 25% of the economy in the last 90 years. Socialists see that the surplus of goods, made available in America by a capitalistic system, keeps growing. And, they want to control a larger percentage of it. However, they don't seem to understand that reducing the incentives of entrepreneurs is likely to disrupt the goose from laying the golden egg. It seems that their successful 90 years of chipping away at the capitalistic system hasn't damaged the goose. So, this experience has just encouraged socialists to continue their past success. And, they have grown more emboldened. They want the whole goose and her eggs!!

Is there room for more compromise (more government) from capitalists? And, is complete socialism the final objective to those (socialists) wanting more governmental control of society. The election of President Trump in 2016 is a good indicator that the right (capitalists) believes that socialism (more freebies for the poor) in America has reached its limits. The Democratic party's economic platform for the 2020 elections is a good indicator that liberals want the country to move much closer to socialism. Therefore, it appears that the battle lines have been formed and the generals should be preparing for war. The time for negotiating a compromise seems to have evaporated.

However, this isn't what the American people want. The call for working together and political compromise can be heard throughout the nation. Most Americans want a united country without the constant verbal assault between political opponents. They don't think that Americans should be fighting each other. With the exception of the Civil War, Americans have been able to resolve their differences amicably to maintain a united America.

Americans have been known for their open-mindedness. Political debate was always a part of the American way of life. It was carried on in the political and social stage, and in party time and dinner time conversation throughout much of American history. This constant political discussion, concerning resolving the problems of the day, helped generate a narrative that was acceptable to all Americans. The tactics of the Democratic party for the last 12 years has made debate toxic, and avoided between most Americans. Breaking down this medium for resolving differences is the main reason for today's divisiveness in America. The political left's intolerance for allowing the expression of any idea that offers an opposing thought (even from their own backers) is responsible for the toxicity that is present in America. Although this tactic is anti-American (against freedom of speech), most Democrats are OK with it, as there has been no backlash from party members.

Facts on which to base different sides of a political position are broadcast by the news media. Except, the set of facts from each political viewpoint are broadcast as falsities by the different leaning political media. So, either the conservative media or the liberal media has to be lying. Hard evidence (having a paper trail) is available, but its context is disputed as having no relevance.

Most Americans prefer to believe their favorite moderator vs. engaging themselves in research. So, the fake news has become an American mental virus that perpetuates the lies though its host. The atmosphere of constant lying or perceived lying by opposing views causes the political hostility never seen in America before. American livelihoods and pocketbooks on the line because they are dependent on the economic philosophy of the political party in power. That fact is drummed home by each party. It is no wonder that political discussions have turned hostile.

Normally, a common sense approach to determining the veracity of facts would lead to an honest conclusion. That's why political debate in the past was used to uncover the truth. The left's successful strategy to shut down debate has worked to prevent their ideas from being exposed as bad for all society, except for the elite socialistic party members. The elite socialists are unwilling to accept challenges to their ideas because their ideas won't stand up in the light of rational thought. Instead, by creating an environment of mob mentality, where criticism of ideas is portrayed as a personal attack on each member of the crowd, these elitists train their crowd to reject any evaluation process. After over 12 years of training their constituents (President Obama's tactics), the Pavlovian instinct has become ingrained. The Philadelphia bell that rings for truth has the opposite effect on today's socialistic followers.

In order for America to unite, the training of the left has to be undone. Changing the psychological behavior of individuals leaning left will be almost impossible, as long as the left's trainers control main stream media and the educators. The right will need to become very confrontational in these arenas to achieve success. Unfortunately, most conservatives believe in the individual's right to choose his own ideas. Aggressively pursuing the change of another's viewpoint isn't conservatism. With this disadvantage, it is hard to see how the leftist mob followers can be converted.

Intelligent conversation won't convert leftists, since it is outlawed by the left. The only thing capable of changing ingrained behavior is a shock to the system. And, that will only happen when the radical base loses everything! Unfortunately, the instigation of bad economic policy will also be horrible for the rest of Americans who were sucked into the morass of bad socialistic governmental policies.

CHAPTER 10

Conclusion

Americans currently have been given a reprieve from the socialistic movement. The election of Donald Trump as president has seriously impeded the progress towards a more powerful American government, run by a select few elitists. Trump's policies have reversed the growth of the power structures (EPA, Obamacare, Department of the Interior, etc.) created by the government to control America. He has dramatically cut government regulations. He has moved the judicial system back to interpreting the Constitution, as it was written, by appointing conservative judges in contrast to the movement to appoint politically motivated judges, He has interfered with the corporate elite's parade of sending American job oversees. And, he has attacked the propaganda machine of leftist mainstream media.

His actions have led to a constant barrage of attacks using false narratives (the Russian conspiracy, collusion with Ukraine, Trump is Putin's puppet, etc.). These attacks are powerful evidence of the elite's push to have President Trump removed from his position of power. The elites don't want a populist movement in America. They are out for their own agenda, not that of the average American. This is true of both Democrats and Republicans. Both parties have spent the last 90 years increasing the power of government through regulation and government spending. They have made politics an extremely successful occupation (Almost all individuals exit the upper branches of government as millionaires). And, they are fearful that an outsider (not a politician) will upset their gravy train. The unethical tactics that they have and are using against Donald Trump will be encountered by any and all strong politicians opposing the elite's status quo. Donald Trump's tweets, 'un-presidential' press conferences, and fights with the 'fake media' are falsely reported as the cause of opposition to him. Instead, it is his lack of tolerance for the elitists, that have been in control of running this country, that have his opponents hating him.

Unfortunately, President Trump will only have another 4+ years of office, if re-elected. It is unlikely that the people will find another individual like him capable of withstanding 4 years of daily onslaught. There have been one after another conspiracies to impeach him. The mainstream media, every minute of every day, broadcasts a constant stream of hate messages about him. Justices thwart his every edict. And, high level government officials leak false information about his conduct.

One must assume that this president is unique and unreplaceable. Therefore, whoever is elected after President Trump's final term will be incapable of continuing to move American power back to the people. Instead, the elite will resume where they left off in 2016. And, socialists will gain power with a 2024 puppet president (ask yourselves why the Democratic party's candidate for president is Joe Biden in 2020 when he is suffering from dementia).

The long run outlook for America is to 'return to the mean'. Americans' standard of living will drop until it becomes normalized with the world. Everything great about America will turn into average. This is what Americans are headed towards very, very, shortly!! The left's group think indoctrination will be successful in recruiting additional percentages of the population, needed to gain ultimate power, to their way of thinking.

Conservatives have to be extremely tough to turn the tide from the path of elitism. And, without a strong man leading the fight, there is no hope.

This book is about socialism and its consequences. Socialism is a cancer that slowly spreads to destroy its host. It has taken deep roots in America. Decay is all around with homeless encampments, a vast amount of drug addicts, criminals with more rights than good people, and America's infrastructure in disrepair.

It's time for all Americans to realize that the American life style is about to drastically change for the worst. The narrative of the left, now winning the minds of many, is that the average American is oppressed, and that he or she is entitled to more of society's output. The oppression part of the narrative is contradicted by the average American's standard of living. The entitlement part is contradicted by the facts of life. There is nothing in life that is free. Only work makes man's necessities available. And, the massive increase in man's work productivity isn't due to the workers but to the entrepreneurs and inventors. So, how can it be rational to argue for more than you've earned through the existing system? In the past, individuals didn't consider health care, advanced education, child care, etc. to be their right. So, what has changed to make it so now?

The left's narrative of oppression and entitlement is an outright lie. What's more, the left's agenda is so bad for the country that it can't stand up to rational debate. Yet, many Americans either chose to believe the garbage they are told. Or, they choose to do nothing about it.

The left wants total control of the country without providing a logical plan, showing that their plan will benefit Americans. And, the methodology of the left has become much more severe since challenged by the election of President Trump. Criminals are let out of jail early, liberal cities don't require society's offenders to post bail before release, black lives matter more than other races, there is a welcome mat for illegal aliens with free social services and sanctuary cities (that protect non-citizens from arrest of any crime), Christianity is under attack while other religions are protected, and on and on. The latest irrational thought of the left is to remove the police from society!!

The truth concerning the continued destruction of America is in plain sight. Yet, hate speech against Trump is more important to liberals than thinking about Democratic proposed policies that will change America into a second rate (at best) country.

The recent policies enacted by liberals are counter to common sense. They are based on the premise that the underprivileged deserve a free pass from society to do whatever and get whatever makes them feel good, as reparations for society's mistreatment of them. However, almost all individuals immigrating to the U.S., before the welfare state, were oppressed people, no matter what their race. Aristocracies and the state had controlled every aspect of their lives. And, reparations were due to the state not to them.

New Americans believed that their own hard work would lead to a better life. And, they bet on it. America succeeded because the repressed used their wit, hard work, and energy to make a better life. They developed their skills to create the greatest economic and political success in the history of the world.

America's current underprivileged have had governmental handouts for close to 60 years. And, that hasn't worked!! Wake up you liberals!!! Force training programs on the poor so that they can become the fishermen discussed in the bible. The easy fix programs of the Democrats, if elected, will succeed in destroying the country. Think about it. Only capitalism provides the incentive and societal structure for revolutionary ideas, that improve productivity, to come to fruition. Only the ignorant would disagree. Unfortunately, their numbers are increasing. Socialism is for dummies!

THE END

APPENDIX OF RECOMMENDED SOURCES

CHAPTER 1 –

1st source - https://www.theatlantic.com/business/archive/2017/09/sweden-startups/541413/

2nd source - https://fee.org/articles/is-sweden-socialist-no-but/

3rd source - https://object.cato.org/sites/cato.org/files/pubs/pdf/pa364.pdf.

CHAPTER 4 –

1st source - https://report.nih.gov/nihfactsheets/ViewFactSheet.aspx?csid=96

2nd source - https://www.cdc.gov/diabetes/statistics/slides/long_term_trends.pdf

3rd source - (https://mises.org/wire/how-government-regulations-made-healthcare-so-expensive

4th source - https://healthpayerintelligence.com/news/gao-3-largest-payers-hold-80-of-private-health-insurance-market

5th source - https://report.ipcc.ch/sr15/pdf/sr15_spm_final.pdf

CHAPTER 5 –

1st source -

https://www.bizjournals.com/bizjournals/washingtonbureau/2016/04/10-regulations-that-give-small-business-owners-the.html

AUTHOR'S REQUEST

America is the greatest country in the world. I fear the radical left will gain control of the country if conservatives don't become very aggressive in defending it. President Trump has been amazing at holding the fort. But, he needs help.

I am donating ½ of the publishing cost of this book to President Trump's campaign. If you think President Trump should extend his term 4 years, please send him a donation.

I would be happy to respond to any comments. My email address is mike.engmann@gmail.com.

Thank you for reading my book.

Sincerely,

Mike Engmann

Lightning Source UK Ltd.
Milton Keynes UK
UKHW010042090223
416653UK00011B/540/J